ISBN: 9781313282079

Published by:
HardPress Publishing
8345 NW 66TH ST #2561
MIAMI FL 33166-2626

Email: info@hardpress.net
Web: http://www.hardpress.net

ZFRM
TYLER

LECTURES

ON

FUTURE PUNISHMENT.

BY EDWARD R. TYLER,
PASTOR OF THE SOUTH CHURCH, MIDDLETOWN, CONN.

" Our God is a consuming fire."
" Am I therefore become your enemy, because I tell you the truth."

MIDDLETOWN, CONN.
PRINTED BY PARMELEE & GREENFIELD.
1829.

DISTRICT OF CONNECTICUT, SS.

[L. S.]   BE IT REMEMBERED, That on the twenty-eighth day of February, in the fifty-third year of the Independence of the United States of America, EDWARD R. TYLER, of the said District, hath deposited in this office the title of a Book, the right whereof he claims as Author, in the words following, to wit :

" *Lectures on Future Punishment. By Edward R. Tyler, Pastor of the South Church, Middletown, Conn.*

" Our God is a consuming fire."

" Am I therefore, become your enemy because I tell you the truth." "

In conformity to the act of Congress of the United States, entitled, " An act for the encouragement of learning, by securing the copies of Maps, Charts and Books, to the authors and proprietors of such copies, during the times therein mentioned." And also to the act, entitled, " An act supplementary to an act, entitled, ' An act for the encouragement of learning, by securing the copies of maps, charts, and books, to the authors and proprietors of such copies during the times herein mentioned,' and extending the benefits thereof to the arts of designing, engraving, and etching historical and other prints."

CHAS. A. INGERSOLL,
Clerk of the District of Connecticut.

A true copy of Record, examined and sealed by me,

CHAS. A. INGERSOLL,
Clerk of the District of Connecticut,

This volume is dedicated to the South Church and Society, in Middletown, by their affectionate Pastor,

EDWARD R. TYLER.

CONTENTS.

LECTURE I.

THE CERTAINTY OF FUTURE PUNISHMENT FROM THE USE OF GEHENNA.

—◦◦◦—

MATTHEW v. 22.

And whosoever shall say, thou fool, shall be in danger of hell-fire.

THE future punishment of the wicked is a doctrine of christianity. A subject of such intense interest and practical importance, cannot be too deeply impressed upon the understanding and heart. Entertaining a firm conviction of this. I cannot feel my duty discharged without laying the evidence of the doctrine before those for whose religious views I am accountable.

I shall first attempt to show. that punishment will be inflicted. leaving the question of its duration for subsequent consideration.

Gehenna, the Hebrew word translated hell in the text, has generally been considered the

2

name of a place of torment in the future world. It originally signified a valley adjacent to Jerusalem, in which the Israelites established the worship of Moloch, under the form of a brazen image, to which they offered their own children in sacrifice, permitting them to fall from the arms of the idol into a furnace of fire. After the captivity, the Jews who regarded this spot with detestation on account of the abominations which had been practised there, threw into it every species of filth, the carcases of animals, and the dead bodies of malefactors. To prevent the pestilence which would be occasioned, if such a mass was left gradually to decay, constant fires were maintained. From this circumstance, the place afterwards assumed the name of the valley of fire. Such then is the primary or original import of Gehenna.

In the time of Christ, however, it had assumed a secondary and metaphorical sense, being employed as the name of a place of torment, in which the Jews believed that demons and the souls of wicked men are to be punished in eternal fire. Nor was it used in any other metaphorical sense. It always denoted the valley of Hinnom, or the place of future punishment. In the Old Testament, it is found in its original import only, and not, as some assert, as an emblem of the destruction of Jerusalem. In the supposed predictions of that event, recorded in the seventh and nineteenth chapters of Jeremiah, Gehenna is mentioned as the theatre of those abominations, for which the city was ultimately to be destroyed. But the Prophet does not make it an emblem of that catastrophe, nor of any other. Nor have I discovered, that the Jews at any period were accustomed to express severe temporal calamities by a metaphorical use of this name. The only secondary sense attached to it in the time of Christ, is that which is adopted by all sound interpreters of the bible. But the most important point, in determining its import in the New Testament, is the manner in which the sacred penmen employ it, or those circumstances of narration, which contribute to unfold its meaning. This must always be the most satisfactory mode of settling the signification of terms, since the same word may be used by different writers in very different senses. No one, however, is allowed to depart from common usage without explaining the *new* sense of his terms. Such an explanation we shall, therefore, find in the texts where Gehenna occurs, or else it must be considered a place of torment in the future state. This view of the case throws the burden of proof upon those who deny it this sense in the New Testament. It devolves upon *them* to prove that Christ departed from popular usage.

With these explanations respecting the meaning of Gehenna both in its original and secondary applications, I proceed to show that in nearly all the passages where it occurs, it can mean only a place of future misery. It has the same metaphorical sense in the New Testament which it had acquired before the christian dispensation commenced.

The text is introduced for the sake of teaching the sinfulness of bad passions and malicious language. Such sins are no less worthy of punishment than those overt acts of disobedience which are commonly acknowledged to be proper subjects of retribution. "Ye have heard that it was said by them of old time; thou shalt not kill, and whosoever shall kill shall be in danger of the judgment; but I say unto you that whosoever is *angry* with his brother without a cause, shall be in danger of the judgment, and whosoever shall *say* to his brother, Raca, shall be in danger of the council, but whosoever shall say, thou fool, shall be in danger of hell-fire." The judgment, it should be remarked, was a court established in each town to take cognizance of offences within its own limits, but having its decisions subject to an appeal to the council or Sanhedrim, the supreme tribunal of the nation. This then appears to be the sense of the text. *Whosoever is angry with his brother without a cause, deserves such a punishment as the judgment is empowered to inflict, and whosoever shall express his anger in words of contempt deserves the vengeance of the Sanhedrim; but whosoever shall say thou miscreant, deserves hell-fire.* That this last expression points to the displeasure of God in the next life is highly probable, because the severest capital punishments peculiar to the Jews were pronounced by the Sanhedrim. And from the manner in which Christ teaches the sinfulness of evil thoughts, it appears that he applies the name hell-fire to some punishment which actually follows disobedience. He admits the propriety of punishing men in these various ways and with various degrees of severity, but contends at the same time, that

2 *

they deserve these penalties, not for overt offences only, but for unlawful words and feelings. He teaches them the spirituality of the law by asserting that the threatenings directed against wicked deeds, respect also the state of the heart, and will actually be executed against the unholy desires and feelings of the mind, of which human law can make no account, and which men are prone to think God will not regard. In doing this he could properly name such punishments only, as were known to be denounced against overt transgression. To illustrate the evil nature of sin in its incipient and immature stages, he would not mention a punishment not known to have been threatened against the most open and flagrant wickedness. It is therefore my firm persuasion, that Christ intended to carry the illustration through all the threatenings denounced against sin. He would say to his disciples, you acknowledge that certain actions justly expose men to punishments in this life and in that which is to come, but I tell you that these wicked actions merely conceived in the heart or expressed by the lips, expose them to the same penalties. But there are additional reasons for supposing that reference is made in the text to future punishment. In proof of this I would refer to the following passages in its immediate neighbourhood. " Whosoever, therefore shall break one of these least commandments and shall teach men so, he shall be called the least in the kingdom of Heaven," that is, shall be excluded from the bliss of the Redeemer's kingdom. " For I say unto you, that except your righteousness shall exceed the righteousness of the scribes and pharisees ye shall in no case enter into the kingdom of Heaven." " Agree with thine adversary quickly, whilst thou art in the way with him, lest at any time the adversary deliver thee to the officer and thou be cast into prison." Exclusion from the kingdom of heaven is in these passages made the penalty of disobedience. The Pharisees and all whose claims to the approbation of God are no better founded, will never participate in the benefits of Christ's death. That the consequences of such an exclusion extend beyond the grave, is apparent from the spiritual nature of the Redeemer's kingdom. The connexion shows that hell-fire denotes the same punishment. But what fixes the sense of Gehenna

in the text with the greatest certainty is its repeated use in the same chapter with more de-
terminate adjuncts. " And if thy right eye offend thee, pluck it out, and cast it from thee:
for it is profitable for thee that one of thy
members should perish, and not that thy
whole body should be cast into *hell*. And if
thy right hand offend thee, cut it off, and cast
it from thee: for it is profitable for thee that
one of thy members should perish and not
that thy whole body should be cast into *hell*."
In these verses it has doubtless the same
meaning as in the text. But before we inquire
what it is, it may be well to explain other expressions here employed. The right hand
and the right eye being those members of the
body which are most highly prized, represent
the objects of this world which we hold most
dear; to offend, means to lead into sin; and the
whole body, in contradistinction to one eye or
one hand the representatives of the dearest
earthly enjoyments, means happiness on the
the largest scale, inclusive of this life and that
which is to come. The sense of the passage
will therefore be this. If the enjoyments of the
world lead you into sin, renounce them, for it
is profitable for you, to be deprived of the en-

joyments of this life, rather than to lose all your happiness in hell. Here, it may be suitable to remark, that our Lord is not speaking of an exposure to be burned alive in the valley of Hinnom, for of that no one was in danger; nor, of exposure to perish in the destruction of Jerusalem, or to lose their *lives* in any other way; for the yielding up of the life is no greater sacrifice than is intended by plucking out an eye, and cutting off a hand, since these members of the body are the representatives of those temporal objects which are dearest to the human heart, among which life is the most conspicuous. Of the principle here involved, the following passage is an admirable illustration. " For whosoever will save his life shall lose it: and whosoever will lose his life for my sake shall find it ;" the sense of which is, that whosoever, through fear of losing his life, shrinks from his duty to Christ, shall lose his happiness beyond the grave, and that whosoever is willing to surrender his life for Christ, shall secure his eternal happiness. It is then nearly certain, that Gehenna is employed in this chapter for a place of punishment in the future state. This is the only sense which meets the necessities of the passage in which it occurs. But let it be admitted, that thus far no certain conclusion in respect to its signification has been obtained. Examine it in other connexions, where the meaning is more decisively fixed. Such an instance is found in the eighteenth chapter of the same gospel. " Wherefore, if thy hand or thy foot offend thee, cut them off and cast them from thee : it is better for thee to enter into life halt or maimed, rather than having two hands or two feet, to be cast into everlasting fire. And if thine eye offend thee, pluck it out and cast it from thee : it is better for thee to enter into life with one eye rather than having two eyes, to be cast into *hell fire*." A part of the language here used has already been explained; the remainder demands our attention. To enter into life is to enter into heaven. Life is often used in this sense. " These shall go away into everlasting punishment, but the righteous into *life* eternal." " And they that are in their graves, shall come forth, some to the resurrection of *life*." "I am the way, the truth and the *life*," the author of eternal happiness. " Because strait is the gate and narrow is the way that leadeth unto *life*," unto eternal happiness. In this place, it can have no other import. It cannot mean the present life, for on that the persons who are addressed have already entered ; it cannot denote any of the enjoyments of this life, of which men will fail unless they sacrifice a right hand or a right eye : for it is said to be better for them to renounce these present objects of affection and desire, rather than to fail of entering into *life*; plainly implying, that they are not the same : nor does it mean, to enter into the kingdom of God, merely as respects its temporal benefits. It may, and doubtless does mean, to enter into the kingdom of God, when that kingdom is viewed as extending beyond the grave. In this sense, to enter into the kingdom of heaven, is to enter into eternal happiness. But if it procures nothing but temporal blessings, and is not indissolubly connected with eternal happiness, to enter into life cannot be a synonymous expression. For, in addition to what has been said, professing the name of Christ did not secure the primitive disciples from losing their lives in as horrid forms as they did, who perished at the seige of Jerusalem. Most of the apostles suffered martyrdom. Nor did all the unbelieving Jews perish in the overthrow of their capital. Yet it seems that entering into life is mentioned as absolute security, and as the only adequate security against being cast into hell or everlasting fire, expressions here used interchangeably. Upon the phrase, " everlasting fire," sufficient will be said in a subsequent lecture on the duration of future punishment. To that I must refer for additional evidence, that Gehenna is the name of a place of torment in the next state. If my hearers should then be satisfied that *everlasting* implies a proper eternity, the controversy is settled. *Endless* fire cannot be the name of any temporal calamity. But the meaning is satisfactorily determined without such corroboration, if to enter into life denotes entering into heaven, or becoming an heir of glory. For the passage under review contains this sentiment;—If any objects of affection or desire lead you into sin, renounce them, for it is better for you to obtain eternal happiness, having surrendered the pleasures of this life, than to be cast into hell, after having possessed them. But the evidence on this subject is not yet exhausted. Indeed, the following passage in the tenth chapter of Matthew, with the parallel one in Luke. more clearly fixes the meaning than any I have yet cited. "And fear not them that kill the body, but are not able to kill the soul: but rather fear him, which is able to destroy both soul and body in hell." Universalists contend, that by the *soul* is here meant the vital principle. But if this is true, while hell denotes no more than some temporal punishment, we shall have the absurdest declaration ever made by man, inspired or uninspired. Fear not them that kill the body, that is, destroy life, but are not able to kill the soul, that is, to destroy the vital principle, but rather fear him which is able to destroy both the vital principle and the life, in the destruction of Jerusalem, or by some other great temporal calamity. Is this no absurdity? Fear not them that destroy the life, but are not able to destroy the life, but rather fear him that is able to destroy the life and the life in the destruction of Jerusalem! But in palliation of such gross contradictions, it is said that the soul in the last clause of the verse is pleonastic, so that the body and the soul mean merely the vital principle, or the life. That is poor aid, however, which brings no relief. If the soul means the vital principle or the life, the absurdity still remains, that the disciples are charged

3

not to fear those who destroy the life, but are
not able to destroy the life, but rather to fear
him, who is able to destroy the life in some
great temporal calamity. _All these difficulties are removed by supposing, what is true,
that the soul means the immortal part of man,
a sense which it often bears. We shall then
have this consistent and impressive sense.
Fear not them, which destroy the life but are
not able to destroy the immortal spirit, but
rather fear him who is able to destroy, or to
make wretched, both the body and the immortal spirit, in hell. The destruction of the
body with the soul, is implied in the doctrine
of the resurrection. This interpretation being
admitted, as it must be, it follows irresistibly,
that gehenna is a place of punishment in a future state; for it denotes something that can
be superadded to the loss of life, or death of
the body. The passage in Luke, to which
reference was just now made, is, if possible,
still more decisive. " And I say unto you, my
friends, be not afraid of them that kill the
body, and after that have no more that they can
do; but I will forewarn you whom ye shall
fear : fear him, which after he hath killed, hath
power to cast into hell : yea, I say unto you,

fear him." The obvious conclusion is, that gehenna denotes a punishment to be inflicted after the calamities of this life are passed. "Fear him, which after he hath killed, hath power to cast into hell." To God belongs the prerogative of punishing the dead. In this respect his power is peculiar. Human rage is an object of dread only in this life. Men can destroy the body, but they cannot destroy the soul. Human and divine power are here put in contrast. the whole force of which consists in the meaning of gehenna. If it is not a place of torment in the future state; man, who can take the life. is as much an object of dread, as God. This view is corroborated, by the manner in which gehenna is introduced in the ninth chapter of Mark, where it occurs in three successive passages, "And whosoever shall offend one of these little ones, that believe in me. it is better for him that a millstone were hanged about his neck, and he were cast into the sea. And if thy hand offend thee, cut it off; it is better for thee to enter into life maimed than having two hands to go into hell, into the fire that never shall be quenched." To go into hell, is here represented to be an evil greater than death. In the third chapter of James, gehenna is used for the wicked confined in it, in the same manner that the names of countries are used for their inhabitants or rulers. " And the tongue is a fire, a world of iniquity; so is the tongue among our members, that it defileth the whole body, and setteth on fire the course of nature, and it is set on fire of hell; ' that is, by Satan and his army of subordinate demons. The apostle, therefore, with great force and propriety, exhorts his readers to resist the devil. He assures them that the wisdom of wicked men, is not from above, that it is earthly, sensual, *devilish.* He makes no such remarks of the valley of Hinnom, for it would be folly, to attribute unlawful excitements and sinful actions to the influence of such a place. In describng the abominations which proceed from the tongue, it might be natural to draw an illustration from the most odious spot, with which the Jews were acquainted; but this was not the apostle's object. He was speaking of the *ungovernable nature* of the tongue and not aiming to define the *exact enormity* of its sins. It is set on fire by hell, not by the valley of Hinnom, but by the powers of evil. They alone possess both the ability and disposition to inflame and corrupt. Those who deny the existence of such beings, must still admit, that the force of the figure depends on their supposed agency. That the tongue is inflamed and actuated by the principles of wicked beings, imaginary or real, whose abode is hell, is the only supposition, which affords the declaration of St. James a suitable and impressive sense. This is the tenth instance, in which gehenna has fallen under our examination, in nine of which, it can mean only a place of torment in the future state. In the other case, it admits this meaning, and when viewed in connexion with the context, requires it. In the two remaining passages where it occurs, both of which are in the twenty-third chapter of St. Matthew, it most probably has the same import. "Wo unto you, Scribes and Pharisees, hypocrites! for ye compass sea and land to make one proselyte, and when he is made, ye make him two-fold more the child of hell (or two-fold more wicked) than yourselves." He soon becomes doubly deserving of the punishment of hell. In the the same discourse it is added;*——" Ye ser-

* Perhaps Christ borrows in this chapter, the language originally descriptive of his final coming and of the future condemnation of the wicked, and applies it metaphorically to the approaching destruction of Jerusalem.

pents, ye generation of vipers, how can ye escape the damnation of hell?" All this, it is said, was to come upon that generation. And no doubt it did. Sufficient proof is given in the interrogative affirmation; "How can ye escape the damnation of hell?" It at least implies, that some powerful obstacle opposed their escape. But from the destruction of Jerusalem, many were delivered. Some of them, it is to be presumed, did not live to witness that catastrophe, some were doubtless in distant parts of the world, and some probably escaped from the very flames of the city. These difficulties are removed by supposing, that Christ had reference to the condemnation consequent upon the destruction of Jerusalem—alluding to that event, only as a prelude to what the unbelieving Jews would suffer. This supposition is the more probable, because the Scribes and Pharisees are said to have incurred, by their peculiar injustice and hypocrisy a severer condemnation. " Wo unto you, Scribes and Pharisees, hypocrites! for ye devour widow's houses, and for a pretence make long prayers; therefore, ye shall receive the greater damnation." But this is not true, if the damnation here mentioned, and which the context shows is the same as the damnation of hell. means only the calamities which were about to happen to the Jewish nation. For in those events, the Pharisees suffered only in common with other citizens, not more severely, nor in exact proportion to their crimes. But it is not essential, that the sense of gehenna should be positively ascertained, in these two instances independently considered. It always *may* mean a place of suffering in the future state, and this in most cases, is demonstrably its sense. It is originally the name of a valley near Jerusalem, the only sense occurring in the Old Testament. In the time of Christ, it had assumed a secondary import. being transferred from its primary application, to denote a place in which it was believed, the wicked are to be forever tormented. This is the only metaphorical sense, in which it appears to have been employed. By a careful examination, this seems to be its universal meaning in the New Testament. We may therefore assert, that the argument from this source in favor of future punishment, is complete and unanswerable. But my hearers may wish to learn. what objections are raised against so plain a conclusion.

1. It is said that gehenna cannot mean a place of punishment in the future state, because it is not found in this sense in the Old Testament. But admitting no such use of the word occurs in the ancient scriptures, does it follow that it is not used by Christ and his disciples in this sense? The New Testament was not commenced, until four hundred years after the old was completed. During this period, there was ample time for words to assume new significations. Such changes are common in all languages. No scholar is unacquainted with this most familiar phenomenon in the history of speech. If therefore, from an examination of the New Testament scriptures, gehenna is found to mean a place of punishment in the future world, we must not refuse our assent, if it has this signification no where else. But when we reflect, that this was the popular use of the word among the Jewish contemporaries of the Messiah, and the sense which fair criticism assigns it in the New Testament, it is extremely weak and impertinent, to say, that since it had not this signification several hundred years before, it never did receive it. Terms in every language become obsolete, and new

terms are substituted in their place, to express
an idea, which was held in common by men
in different ages. In each successive generation, both written and oral language receives
modifications in sense, which in process of
time totally change it. Surely, if in the Old
Testament, future punishment is expressed in
other langnage, *Christ* might have applied this
new term in speaking of it. The Jews of that
day believed in a place of future punishment:
to this they applied the name gehenna. Their
belief was in this respect correct. When
speaking, therefore, on the same doctrine,
Christ would be apt to use the language ex-
pressive of it, with which they were familiar,
and about which there was no ambiguity.
The case is somewhat like that of a christian
missionary, who, in translating the Scriptures
into the language of a barbarous people, employs as a name of hell, not a new term, but
one which they had been accustomed to use
in speaking of the abode of the wicked. By
doing this he would tell them, that they had
not been mistaken in believing in such a
place, that it is a doctrine of Christianity as
well as of Paganism; and he would leave them
to learn from other sources the difference be-

tween the doctrine, as taught in the bible and
as it stands in their fables. So our Lord, by
using gehenna in this sense, teaches his disciples that the common opinion in respect to
future rewards and punishments, is true, while
he also admits the propriety of the name. This
is obvious and rational. Nor in saying it, do
we rely at all on the opinions of Zoroaster,
of the unbelieving Jews, or of the authors
of the Apocrypha or of the Talmud. In
proof of the doctrine of future punishment,
we say, that such was the faith, correct or in-
correct, of the Jews in the time of our Lord,
and that gehenna was used as the name of the
place of torment; whence we have a satisfactory reason for Christ's using it as he did.
He did not teach the doctrine, because any
fallible men had received it. It is a part of
his own religion, a truth common to Christianity and to nearly all the religions of men.
Gehenna was a word in use, as a name of the
place of torment, and in this sense we have
seen he employs it.

2. But it is further said, that the doctrine of
future punishment is not taught in the Old
Testament, in any language whatever. The
assertion however is not true. The doctrines,

not only this but others, are taught less explicitly in the Old Testament than in the New; but still, future punishment is taught even there. So at least thought the writers of the Talmud, who abundantly teach it. And what is the import of such language as this? "The wicked shall be turned into hell and all the nations that forget God." If it means no more than that the wicked shall be turned into the *grave*, they might retort: the righteous shall be turned into hell and all the nations that remember God. But should it be admitted, that future punishment is not taught in the Old Testament, does it follow that it cannot be taught in the New? Admirable powers of logic! Of what value is the New Testament, if nothing can be believed, unless first taught in more ancient scriptures. Accordcording to the principles of the objector, the plainest and most important doctrines of Christ, are not to be believed or may be easily controverted, because they are either not mentioned or only obscurely hinted at, in the Old Testament. Unbelievers have only to raise doubts in respect to these hints, and their task will be accomplished. The plainest assertions of the New Testament, must be rejected as unintelligible, or as allusions to Pagan errors, or as mis-translations of the original sense. It is however demonstrably certain, that the doctrine of future punishment is revealed in the Old Testament. This objection is also incompatible with the preceding. Christ could not have obtained, from the Old Testament, a name applied to the place of torment, if future punishment is not there revealed. A new doctrine requires a new term. or one employed in a new sense.

3. There are but two other considerations, which can, with any plausibility, be urged against the result of the foregoing examinations. Nor are they of much force. They only need to be noticed, because they are often and imposingly advanced. In the instances in which gehenna is undeniably used, in the sense of a place of torment in the future state, it is found in discourses addressed to the disciples of our Lord, and not to the unbelieving Jews. who were most exposed. Whereas, in modern times, impenitent sinners and not Christians, are addressed with these terrible denunciations. The manner of our Savior. it is said, indicates, that the disciples were more exposed to gehenna than other

men. In reply, it may be demanded, why he did not warn unbelievers, rather than his disciples, provided gehenna denotes the approaching destruction of Jerusalem. For on this, as well as on the other supposition, unbelievers were in greater danger than his disciples. When that event took place. the apostles were scattered over the Roman empire, preaching the gospel. But there is an adequate reason for teaching his immediate followers, and the future heralds of the cross, the doctrine of future punishment. He was preparing them for their work, by telling them in the ear, what they were commanded to proclaim upon the house-tops. In this, there was an important use, while perhaps he knew, that warnings, addressed to the unbelieving Jews, would be entirely lost.

4. The remaining objection is more plausible, but equally futile. The disciples of Christ never used gehenna. except in a single instance, in their epistles to the churches. He commanded them, to proclaim his instructions upon the house-tops, but they do not mention a place of torment, under this name. To which it may be replied;—" By writing and circulating the gospels, containing the

history of our Lord, and of his most private instructions, they did proclaim to the world, what they were taught in secret." The objector overlooks this circumstance. He seems to suppose, that the disciples never discharged the commission, to proclaim upon the house-tops, what they had heard in the ear, if future punishment is not taught in their epistles and in the very language of his discourses. But they did discharge it, by writing and circulating the gospels. Nor do we know, what was the ordinary style of apostolic preaching. We have only a few examples given in the acts of the apostles, and in them we find evident traces of the doctrine of future punishment. As in the reply of Peter to the interrogation of the vast multitude, assembled on the day of Pentecost,—" Men and brethren what shall we do?" He understands them to inquire, what they shall do for the remission of their sins, and directs them to repent. Their sense of guilt and exposure, could not certainly have resulted from an apprehension of temporal evils. Their crime had exposed them to none. The same may be inferred from Paul's address to Felix ;—" As he reasoned of righteousness. temperance and judgment to come, Felix trembled." It was not the fear of any present danger, that made this hardened man tremble before a preacher of the cross. And probably, in all their oral instructions, the doctrine of future punishment held a sufficiently conspicuous place. But in the brief history, which we have of their first labors, and in their epistles, written for the sake of exposing certain errors, correcting certain abuses, and elucidating and enforcing the abstruser doctrines of religion, it was not to be expected, that the first and plainest truth of christianity, should be formally stated and proved. It was every where taken for granted by them. Most of those, to whom they wrote, were in possession of one or more of the gospels. None of them doubted the doctrine of future punishment. There was no call, therefore, for an epistle, designed to refute the notion of universal salvation. Almost all the epistles, are written upon general questions, the decision of which does not necessarily require any allusion to the retributions of another world. Would it be strange, if, in writing a letter to a friend on church government, you should say nothing of the resurrection of the body? If in such a letter, you should say nothing on the subject of future punishment, would it be right for your friend to infer, that you are an universalist? Yet this is the reasoning of those, who say, that Paul was an universalist, because, when writing on other subjects, he has not quoted St. Matthew on future punishment! But though the nature of the case did not require, that this subject should be designedly treated of, in portions of the New Testament devoted to other topics, yet it will hereafter be made to appear, that the apostles recognize future punishment, as a doctrine of christianity. Should it again be asked, why they did not use the name gehenna, when speaking of future punishment, the answer is evident. If our Savior taught the doctrine at all, he did it almost constantly and in a great variety of forms, while he uses gehenna in only four or five of his discourses. When this is considered, the single instance in which it is used by James, seems to afford it a fair share of notice, especially since most of the first readers of the epistles, were not Jews but Gentiles, to whom other designations of the place of future punishment were more familiar. Thus it appears, that no objection exists to the conclusion, established in this discourse.

I have now closed this outline of the argument, in favor of future punishment, from the use of gehenna in the New Testament. The obvious inference is, that some men will be miserable after death. The existence of heaven, is sufficient proof of its being the residence of happy spirits. An analogous conclusion is drawn from the existence of a place of punishment. It is inhabited. Indeed, so long as it is acknowledged, that faith in Christ is the only security against destruction in hell, it cannot be questioned, that many are involved in it. It cannot be believed, that all the dead chose to serve God in their life time, at the hazard of losing the dearest earthly objects. This is not the case with all the living, even in this enlightened and religious age. How many, as far as the eye can follow them, even to the verge of eternity, bear the marks of the most decided impiety! But this point need not be argued. There is a hell, in which incorrigible sinners are punished.

LECTURE II.

THE CERTAINTY OF FUTURE PUNISHMENT FROM THE USE OF HADES.

LUKE xvi. 23.

And in hell, he lifted up his eyes, being in torments.

THE Greek poets divide *Hades* into two apartments, one of which they call *Tartarus*, where the wicked dwell in great degradation and misery, the other *Elysium*, the delightful residence of the righteous. The latter Jews, many of whom were better acquainted with the Greek than with the Hebrew language, adopted the same meaning, with only slight modifications. They supposed hades to be a vast subterranean receptacle, in which the souls of men exist in a separate state, until the resurrection of their bodies. According to them, the region of the blessed, called paradise in allusion to their own scriptures, is in the upper part of this receptacle; while beneath is the abyss, in which the souls of the wicked are subjected to punishment. Thus it appears, they sometimes used it in a more extensive sense than they attached to gehenna, which denotes only the place of torment, or that part of hades where the wicked are confined. That these are the views, which the contemporaries of Christ, both Jews and Gentiles, entertained, no one disputes. In the New Testament, the same signification prevails. But hades does not always include both apartments or divisions of the receptacle. It most frequently denotes, either the place of torment or paradise, and not ordinarily both at once. The reason of this, is, that persons, who are mentioned, as dwelling or destined to dwell there, are decidedly fitted for the region of the blessed, or for the abyss of woe, and cannot be spoken of as inhabiting both. When the wicked are said to descend to hades, that part of it is intended, which is called by the Greeks tartarus, and by the Hebrews gehenna; but when the righteous descend thither, it is to elysium or paradise. Thus, on one occasion, it is said in reference to Christ, that his soul was not left in *hades ;* and on another, that the rich man also died, and in *hades* he lifted up his eyes, being in torments. Both declarations are true. Christ and the rich man descended to hades, but not to the same apartment; one went to paradise with the penitent thief, the other went to be tormented in gehenna. Lazarus was carried by angels to Abraham's bosom, another name of the region of bliss, while the angels, who kept not their first estate, were cast down to tartarus, that part of hades in which the wicked are tormented.

It seems, on the authority of these facts, that an invincible argument, in favor of future punishment, may be drawn from the use of hades. But it is objected, that it most commonly means the grave, and that, when it will not bear this signification, it is not demonstrably a place of torment. Such assertions are easily made, and greedily credited by multitudes, which renders it necessary to notice all the passages, in which the word occurs. We first meet with it, in the eleventh chapter of Matthew. " And thou Capernaum, which art exalted unto heaven, shalt be brought down to hell." This is repeated in Luke;—" And thou, Capernaum, which art exalted to heaven, shalt be thrust down to hell." In these places, hades is probably used for that part, where lost men are tormented. On this supposition, the declaration of Christ to the inhabitants of Capernaum, is this;—*Your privileges have been great. I have given you, every suitable evidence of my divine mission, but you have rejected me. Your trial is now completed. You must be thrust down to hell.* But this is not certainly his meaning. In speaking of their privileges and prosperity, he compares them in their exaltation to heaven; in speaking, therefore, of their impending calamities and ruin as a city, he might aptly compare the extent of their fall with the world of departed spirits, which, according to Jewish notions, is the lowest imaginable place. But on this supposition, the strength and liveliness of the figure, depends upon the primary and proper meaning of hades. Our Lord tells them, you are exalted very high, even to heaven, but you shall be thrust down very low, even to hades. The grave cannot be intended. In the sixteenth chapter of Matthew, the word again occurs. "I say also unto thee, that thou art Peter; and upon this rock, I will build my church, and the gates of *hades* shall not prevail against it." Here, it is used for Satan and his subordinate demons, the inhabitants of tartarus. Christ promises, that the powers of evil shall not destroy his church. Were hades the grave, the figure would have neither force nor beauty. It is obvious, without a declaration, that the grave cannot undermine christianity. It is quite absurd, to charge it with such an intention. But the world of wicked spirits, used, by a common figure, for its inhabitants, is a most malignant and powerful adversary to the cause of truth. The next passage, which we notice, is in the fifteenth chapter of the first epistle to the Corinthians. "Oh death where is thy sting? Oh grave (oh hades) where is thy victory?" The apostle is speaking of the resurrection. He mentions Christ, as the author. What, then, is implied in the resurrection, or over what powers does Christ triumph in accomplishing that event? He resuscitates the body, which is held in the chains of death, and recalls the soul from the receptacle of the dead, to re-unite it to the body. These are the powers, alluded to in the text;—"Oh death, where is thy sting? Oh hades, where is thy victory?" The passage, therefore, is incumbered with no difficulty, on assigning to hades, the meaning which it bore in Greek usage. This interpretation, however, is not the one, which appears most satisfactory. The apostle probably did not intend to convey, more than one idea by the expressions;—"Oh death where is thy sting, Oh grave where is thy victory?" After having explained the glorious resurrection, which Christ has procured for his followers, he triumphantly inquires, where is the victory of sin, or of the powers arrayed against the christian? He declares, that the sting of death, or that, which renders death terrible, is sin. Over this, Christ has completely triumphed. By obtaining, for his disciples, an inheritance in heaven, of which their resurrection is the first fruits, he has disappointed sin, and deprived it of its prey. This explanation attaches to death and hades, the same sense, and supposes, that they are put by metonymy, for the authors of death, or for satan and his angels. the inhabitants of hades. Besides the passages already alluded to, in which the word occurs, we find it four times in the Apocalypse of St. John;—"I am he that liveth and was dead; and behold I am alive forevermore, Amen; and have the keys of *hades* and of death." Keys are an emblem of power. Christ asserts his authority, not over death and the grave, for that would be mere tautology, but over death and all those, who have passed into the unseen state. It is not used in this place, in a sense which is inconsistent with its having, for a primary and literal meaning, the mansion or world of the dead. "And I looked and behold a pale horse, and his name that sat on him was death : and *hades* followed with him." Death on a pale horse, is an emblem of a destructive pestilence. But it is not so easy, to determine the signification of hades. It probably means, that vast multitudes became victims of the disease, or were drawn down to the mansions of the dead. This is a sense, which suits the passage, and which renders it altogether unnecessary, to apply to hades a different meaning from that, which it ordinarily bears. " And I saw the dead, small and great, stand before God : and the books were opened : and another book was opened, which is the book of life, and the dead were judged out of those things, which were written in the books, according to their works. And the sea gave up the dead, which were in it ; and death and *hades* delivered up the dead, which were in them : and they were judged every.man accord-

ing to their works." This is an account of the
last judgment. The dead all appeared before
the tribunal of Christ. The sea and death and
hades gave up the dead which were in them.
This is a familiar mode of expressing a general
resurrection. All who had suffered death
from any cause whatever, appeared before the
judgment seat, "And they were judged every
man according to their works.' By this it is
not determined, whether hades means the
mansion of the dead, or simply the grave. It
is only affirmed, that there was a general
resurrection of men, whether they had perished in the sea or by disease, or in some other
form But it is immediately added. that death
and hades were cast into the lake of fire. This,
it has been supposed means, that no death
shall occur after the judgment day. Such an
interpretation, however, poorly accords with
the succeeding declaration,—" This is the second death." For if casting death and hades
into the lake of fire only denotes, that those
who had once been victims of them. shall
never be again, there is no propriety in calling it the second death. Another interpretation is much better. Death is put for the authors of death, and hades, for the inhabitants

5

of tartarus, for Satan and all the enemies of Christ. The authors of death and the powers of darkness are thus represented as cast into the lake of fire. "This is the second death."*

All the passages in which hades occurs in the New Testament have now been noticed. In every instance it has reference, more or less direct, to the mansions of the dead. In cases where it is used figuratively, the force of the language depends upon this literal and primary sense. But in this examination, the most important paragraph in which it is found, requires more consideration. I refer to the parable of the rich man and Lazarus in the sixteenth chapter of Luke. The Pharisees had overheard a discourse in which Christ had taught his disciples the impossibility of serving God and mammon; and being covetous, they derided him. In illustration of what he had said he tells them,—" There was a certain rich man, which was clothed in purple and fine linen, and fared sumptuously every day: and there was a certain beggar named Lazarus which was laid at his gate,

* See Eichhorn on Revelations.

full of sores, and desiring to be fed with the crumbs which fell from the rich man's table: moreover, the dogs came and licked his sores. And it came to pass, that the beggar died, and was carried by angels into Abraham's bosom. The rich man also died, and was buried: And in hell he lifted up his eyes, being in torments, and seeth Abraham afar off, and Lazarus in his bosom. And he cried, and said, Father Abraham, have mercy on me and send Lazarus, that he may dip the tip of his finger in water, and cool my tongue: for I am tormented in this flame." By this he teaches them, what is the consequence of relying upon riches. Men who serve wealth, or seek their supreme good in it, cannot serve God. The consequence is, that after death, they will be sent into a place of misery; while many of the poor, who were not under such a temptation, will be admitted to a happy life. Whether Dives and Lazarus are fictitious persons or not, is immaterial, in deciding the sense which the sacred writers have attached to hades. No hypercriticism has ever been able to explain this parable, so as to weaken the evidence which it affords in favor of future punishment. In accordance with this undeniable example, hades may be translated the abode of the dead, except in a few passages where it is used figuratively, and in evident allusion to this sense. In confirmation of this, I would refer to an additional source of evidence. The sacred writers employ, in the place of hades, a word which they considered precisely synonymous. In our version, it is rendered, the *deep*, the *pit*, the *bottomless pit*. It occurs in the tenth chapter of Romans. " But the righteousness which is of faith, speaketh on this wise : say not in thine heart, who shall ascend into heaven ? that is, to bring Christ down from above : or, who shall descend into the deep? that is, to bring Christ up again from the dead?" When the Jews wished to describe any thing as above human power, they compared it with the impossibility of ascending into heaven, or of descending into the deep, the receptacle of the dead. The apostle declares, that no such impossibility attends salvation by faith. St. Luke also informs us, that a legion of devils besought Christ not to command them to go into the *deep*. The word occurs repeatedly in Revelations. " And the fifth angel sounded, and I saw a star fall from heaven unto the earth :

and to him was given the key of the *bottom-less pit*. And he opened the *bottomless pit;* and there arose a smoke out of the *pit*, as the smoke of a great furnace." The passages, therefore, in which this name is found, may be employed in the argument, in connexion with those in which hades is the term of designation.

There is no reply, which can be made to the conclusion, at which we have arrived, unless it is, that hades in the version of the Seventy, and the corresponding word in the Hebrew bible, never mean the world of departed spirits. That such an objection is unfounded, the following passages from the Old Testament clearly show. " Hades from beneath is moved for thee, to meet thee at thy coming. It stirreth up the dead for thee, even all the chief ones of the earth : it hath raised up from their thrones all the kings of the earth." This is the song of triumph on the fall of the king of Babylon. It represents the dead as assembled in one place, and all the kings of the earth as rising up to meet the tyrant. We have instances too of the opposition, in which heaven for height, and hades for depth, were conceived to stand to each other, which is entirely incon-

5 *

sistent with the opinion, that the word in the Old Testament always denotes the grave. "Canst thou by searching find out God? Canst thou find out the Almighty unto perfection? It is high as heaven, what canst thou do? deeper than hades; what canst thou know?" Surely they might have looked into the grave. "If I ascend up into heaven, thou art there: If I make my bed in hades, behold thou art there." "Though they dig into hades, thence will my hand take them: though they climb up to heaven, thence will I bring them down." "A fire is kindled in mine anger, and shall burn to the lowest hades." The force of the figure depends upon hades being the lowest conceivable place, or a very low place in the earth, where both Jews and Greeks supposed the mansion of the dead to be situated. To check the presumption of Job, God inquires of him;—"Have the gates of death been opened unto thee, or hast thou seen the doors of the shadow of hades?" This challenge shows, that the grave, the doors of which are accessible to men, is not the subject of discourse. "The wicked shall be turned into *hades*, and all the nations that forget God." Not only the wicked but the righteous are

turned into the grave, yet both do not descend
to hell. But were hades used in the Old
Testament for the place of departed spirits,
there would be no valid argument against
its having this sense in the New. We find it in
the writings of the Apostles. We ask its
meaning. The abettor of universal salvation
replies, that in the Old Testament it always
denotes the grave. But on reading the gospels,
we discover. that persons live and act in it. If
therefore it means the grave in the Hebrew
scriptures, it must have another signification,
which will suit the descriptions given of it
in the New Testament. *There*, in several
instances at least. it obviously means the
mansion of the dead. It is consequently
trifling with our understandings, to say, that
it sometimes signifies the grave, which may
be true, while it sometimes means a place of
punishment beyond the grave.

This investigation in my own judgment es-
tablishes the conclusion of the last lecture,
that some men will be subjected to punishment in the future state. In the pursuit of
this truth, its solemn and momentous import
has not escaped my mind. Though the subject has demanded the undivided and unim-

passioned mind of the critic, yet the thought
has not failed to arise as those passages, which
disclose the fates of men, have passed in review, that you and I are travelling to eternity,
and that we are personally concerned in the
awful fact which has been unfolded. The
reflection is not easily eluded, that the privileges which we enjoy may be abused and involve us in deeper misery. Capernaum once
exalted to heaven, is now thrust down to hell.
They who despised Moses' law died without
mercy; of how much sorer punishment shall
he be thought worthy, who rejects the gospel?
The man who was clothed in purple and fine
linen and fared sumptuously every day, has
closed his career of pride and luxury, and in
hell he lifts up his eyes being in torments.
Perhaps one of my own beloved congregation
is ripening for such a fate. Perhaps he is
guilty of covetousness that gross idolatry;
perhaps he is fascinated by pleasure; perhaps
he is held by some great but worldly ambition;
perhaps he is bewildered by error; perhaps
some iron handed vice is subduing him to the
dominion of satan; perhaps, if no other foe
assails him, stupidity and procrastination are
hurrying his soul into the pit. This possibili-

ty is a solemn and overwhelming truth. Painful as the admission is, it cannot be withheld. To deny it would subserve no valuable purpose, but would involve me, in the condemnation of a false witness, and you in the anguish of disappointment. God has given us this life, in which to prepare for the next. What folly then is superior to his, who bends all his efforts to the desires of this world. who bounds his vision by the limits of time? Will it avail any thing in the day of Jesus Christ, that he refused instruction and despised reproof? that he listened not to the monitions of the spirit and word of God, nor to the appeals of conscience. nor to the preaching of the cross? And who will be able to screen the naked spirit of that false ambassador of Christ, who fearful of giving momentary pain or of incurring the hatred of men, allows his hearers to be ignorant of their exposure or insensible of it? The awful truth, that nothing will protect the unfaithful, should never be forgotten. A little while hence, an account of my stewardship will be demanded. Then at the tribunal of Jesus Christ, we must stand together. The books will be opened and out of them we shall be judged. Among other things there recorded, is the history of my ministry! Do not then demand of me a mode of preaching, which suits the carnal mind. There too. are your lives with every thought, word and action, distinctly traced! Then demand not. that I should feed your hopes of impunity in sin, and lull you into a false security. Remember, another book will be opened, which is the book of life. and whosoever is not found written therein will be cast into the lake of fire. Let not this assembly break up without solemnly inquiring, where and with whom you will soon assemble. Where? Not in a world of probation. With whom? Not in a mixed company of christians and unbelievers. But you will either rise to the fruition of heavenly society and occupations, or descend into the abyss with satan and his angels. Inquire, to which of these states are your characters most suited. How would the all engrossing question be decided. were you now to die? In what place would you appear. in Paradise or in Gehenna? Does conscience decide against you? Oh my hearer, remember the Lamb of God, which taketh away the sins of the world! Trust in him, and then you may triumphantly exclaim: Oh death, where is thy sting? Oh *hades*, where is thy victory?

LECTURE III.

MATTHEW vii. 13, 14.

Enter ye in at the strait gate; for wide is the gate, and broad is the way that leadeth to destruction, and many there be which go in thereat: because strait is the gate, and narrow is the way, which leadeth unto life, and few there be that find it.

In pursuing the subject of the preceding lectures, it is important to call your attention to various additional passages and forms of expression, in which the doctrine of future punishment is taught; since nothing is more usual than to censure ministers of the gospel, for frequently speaking of a world, the name of which is found only twenty-three times in the New Testament. The text first solicits our notice. The *life* of which Christ here speaks, is *eternal* life or happiness in heaven.

That this is the usual meaning of the word in such connexions, has once been shown. "What good thing shall I do, that I may have *eternal life?*" "If thou wilt enter into *life*, keep the commandments." "Then hath God also to the Gentiles. granted repentance unto *life.*" "I am the bread of *life:* he that cometh to me, shall never thirst." "Search the scriptures; for in them ye think ye have *eternal life:* and they are they which testify of me. And ye will not come to me, that ye might have *life.*" The text then declares, that on account of the difficulty of discovering the way to heaven, many walk in that which leads to destruction. Eternal life and destruction are opposed to each other, and denote different states of existence; the one of unsullied character and of unalloyed enjoyment—the other of complete moral ruin and wretchedness. Such a figurative use of *destruction* is common in all languages. It is frequent in the bible. "Pride goeth before destruction," not annihilation, but the ruin of one's character and peace. "Oh Israel, thou hast destroyed thyself." "Destroy not him with thy meat" "Punished with everlasting destruction." Agreeably to this use, the words of Christ contain the following solemn exhortation. *Enter in at that strait gate, which leads to eternal happiness; for wide is the gate and broad is the way, which leads to the miseries of the wicked in hell; because strait is the gate and narrow is the way which leads to eternal happiness, and few there be that find it.* The supposition that " *destruction*" denotes the calamities which were soon to befall the Jewish nation, cannot be sustained. The miseries spoken of are such as happen to those, and those only, who enter not into eternal happiness ; whereas, on the scheme of universal salvation, those who perished in the destruction of Jerusalem found the way to heaven, as truly as those who escaped. But it is sometimes said, that *life* in the text means the kingdom of Christ, considered simply as a temporal kingdom; and that all who became its subjects were to be saved from the destruction of Jerusalem, while those who would not recognize the Messiah, were to perish. Such is the disposition of men to reduce the benefits of christianity, to the melioration of their temporal condition ! This, the Jews did—this universalists do now. We must believe, according to these interpreters, that the object of Christ's untiring admonitions and warnings, was to save a little band of men from the flames of Jerusalem! But have they forgotten, what our Lord declares, that if half the mighty works, which he did in Capernaum, had been done in Tyre and Sidon, they would have continued to this day? Why then did he not save these cities, rather than Capernaum? If his object was to deliver a few persons from temporal calamities, his success would have been much greater in the cities of the plain. There, according to his own declaration, he would have produced a general reformation, while in Jerusalem, he gained only a few disciples. He might have reasons for not entering on his mission to save the world from spiritual evils, sooner than he did; but if his object was to rescue a few men from such a calamity as the destruction of a city, the best opportunity was not selected. He did not save Jerusalem, nor the great body of its inhabitants, nor the other cities of Judea, where his works were performed; yet he says, that had he appeared for the cities of the plain, they would have repented and continued prosperous. Universalists, however, tell us, that all the terrible denunciations, with which he closes most of his parables, and

which he intersperses in all his instructions,
relate to the approaching ruin of Jerusalem:
and among the rest, we must believe. that the
text is of this description. There is. however,
not only an improbability on the face of their
assertion, but it is wholly unsustained. *Life*
no where means an enjoyment of the temporal privileges of the true church. To enter
into life, may denote entering into the kingdom of God, when this last expression is used
for heaven, but in no other case. Though
enough has been said to establish the proof,
which the text affords, of future punishment,
yet I cannot forbear adverting to the unanswerable confirmation. furnished by an analogous passage in the thirteenth chapter of St.
Luke. "Then said one unto him, Lord, are
there few that be saved?" What is the import of this inquiry? saved from what? from
the destruction of Jerusalem? The answer
of Christ will determine. "And he said unto
them, strive to enter in at the strait gate; for
many, I say unto you, will seek to enter in and
shall not be able. When once the master of
the house is risen up and hath shut to the
door, and ye begin to stand without and to
knock at the door, saying, Lord, Lord, open

unto us; and he shall answer, I say unto you, I know you not whence ye are : then shall ye say; we have eaten and drunk in thy presence and thou hast taught in our streets. But he shall say, I tell you, I know you not whence ye are : depart from me all ye workers of iniquity. There shall be weeping and gnashing of teeth, when ye shall see Abraham and Isaac and Jacob and all the prophets in the kingdom of God, and you yourselves thrust out." The figure of shutting to the door, seems to refer to the close of probation; and the banishment of the workers of iniquity, from the presence of Christ, when seeking for admission, is utterly inexplicable, on any supposition, but that of a final judgment. But what should set the subject at rest, is the closing representation ;—"And there shall be weeping and gnashing of teeth, when ye shall see Abraham and Isaac and Jacob in the kingdom of God, and you yourselves thrust out." This, as well as the other facts here stated, has not yet taken place, and can be fulfilled only at the close of the world. Then, and not till then, shall they " come from the east and from the we.t and from the north and from the south," out of all nations, " and sit down in the kingdom of God." This account must not only be regarded, as an illustration of the views which have been taken of the text, but also, as an independent proof of future punishment.

2. " The Son of man shall send forth his angels, and they shall gather out of his kingdom all things which offend and them that do iniquity ; and shall cast them into the furnace of fire : there shall be wailing and gnashing of teeth." This seems to be sufficiently explicit and intelligible, especially if we read in connexion with it the following text. " So shall it be at the end of the world ; the angels shall come forth and sever the wicked from among the just, and shall cast them into the furnace of fire : there shall be wailing and gnashing of teeth." This too, it is said, relates to the destruction of Jerusalem, at which time the Jews ceased to be a nation. But in that event the declaration was not accomplished, that the wicked shall be separated from the just, and that all things which offend shall be gathered out of Christ's kingdom. Not to say, that this is predicted to take place

Math. xiii. 41, 42, 49, 50,
6 *

at the *end* of the world, which it will be difficult to prove, means the end of the Jewish
state; it is obvious, that Christ has never yet
gathered out of his kingdom, all things which
offend and them which do iniquity. It should
also be noticed, that *gehenna* and the *furnace of
fire* are synonymous expressions.

3. " Many shall come from the east and
west and shall sit down with Abraham, Isaac
and Jacob, in the kingdom of heaven. But the
children of the kingdom (the Jews who had
enjoyed the privileges of the kingdom of God
on earth) shall be cast into outer darkness:
there shall be weeping and gnashing of teeth."
The kingdom of heaven in this place, manifestly means the heavenly world. When
many of the Gentiles are admitted into it, in
company with the pious ancestors of the
Jews, they themselves are to be cast into
outer darkness, where they are to suffer the
most excruciating torments. The representation of men coming from all parts of the
earth, and entering in.o the immediate society of the patriarchs, while the unbelieving
children of the visible church are cast

Math. viii. 11 12.

into a dark and miserable place by themselves, is not applicable to any events, which have taken place in this world. In the fifth chapter of St. John, the same fact is differently expressed. " Marvel not at this: for the hour is coming, in the which all that are in the graves shall hear his voice, and shall come forth; they that have done good, unto the resurrection of life ; and they that have done evil, unto the resurrection of damnation." Punishment, is not only the sense of *damnation*, most agreeable to common usage, but which the construction of this sentence requires. While some of the dead are raised to immortal happiness, others will come forth to the resurrection of damnation. They are not annihilated. nor admitted to heaven, but are condemned and punished.

4. At the same conclusion we arrive, by examining that large class of passages, which develope the principles on which the destinies of men will be decided. " But I say unto you, that every idle word that men shall speak, they shall give account thereof, in the day of judgment. For by thy words thou shalt be

justified and by thy words thou shalt be condemned." This is applied to men generically, to every generation, both of Jews and Gentiles. "And his Lord was wroth, and delivered him to the tormentors, till he should pay all that was due unto him. So likewise shall my Heavenly Father do also unto you, if ye from your hearts forgive not every one, his brother their trespasses." "For this we know, that no unclean person, nor covetous man, who is an idolater, hath any inheritance in the kingdom of Christ and of God. Let no man deceive you with *vain words*, for because of these things cometh the wrath of God, upon the children of disobedience." "Now the works of the flesh are manifest, which are these; adultery, fornication, uncleanness, lasciviousness, idolatry, witchcraft, hatred, variance, emulations, wrath, strife, seditions, heresies, envyings, murders, drunkenness, revellings and such like; of which I tell you before, as I have also told you in time past, that they which do such things shall not inherit the kingdom of God." What it is, to inherit the kingdom of God, we are informed in an ac-

Math. xviii. 34,—5. Eph. v. 5, 6. Gal. v. 19, 21.

count of the last judgment. " Come ye blessed of my Father, inherit the kingdom prepared for you from the foundation of the world."
It is to possess the rewards of the righteous
in heaven. In the foregoing quotations, the
assertion is unequivocally made, that certain
sins unabandoned, will terminate in an exclusion from the blessings of salvation. The argument, derived from them in favor of future punishment, is grounded upon the historical fact,
that many persons enter the grave, with the
characters described. It cannot be supposed,
that they who give no signs of repentance until
the very crisis of death. then invariably become
the subjects of so great a change; especially
when it is recollected, how many are suddenly
arrested in the midst of their crimes, and destroyed without a moment's reflection. The
threatening against such persons must be executed. Is not this an obvious conclusion from
the reiterated declaration, that sinners of every
description shall be excluded from heaven,
and visited with the wrath of God, when it is
known, that they often die, as they live, to every
good work reprobate ? " Then said Jesus
unto them, I go my way, and ye shall seek
me, and *shall die in your sins :* whither I go,

ye cannot come." "I said therefore unto you, that ye shall die in your sins : for if ye believe not that I am he, ye shall die in your sins." " Ye shall seek me, and shall not find me : and where I am, thither ye cannot come." These passages, addressed to the unbelieving Jews, are as decisive as any can be, in proof of future punishment. They do not, indeed, at first sight, wear this aspect. It is only by an acquaintance with the nature of Christianity, as a system for restoring man to the favor of God through the forgiveness of sins, that we see the force of the denunciation ;—" *Ye shall die in your sins*." Such a death is indissolubly connected with punishment. Indeed, in most of our Lord's addresses to the Jews, he charges them with an opposition to himself, fatal to their souls. " How can ye believe, who receive honor one of another." " Whither I go ye cannot come." The very circumstance. that faith in Christ is made essential to salvation, connected with the final rejection of him by the Jews, is complete demonstration of the doctrine of future punishment. It does not show in what future punishment

John viii. 21, 24. vii. 34.

consists. A knowledge of this, we must gather from other sources. But it does show, that some men will not inherit the kingdom of Christ and of God. "I pray for them: I pray not for the world, but for them which thou hast given me." " Neither pray I for these alone; but for them also which shall believe on me through their word." For the world, (under that appellation Christ includes all final unbelievers) he does not pray: but only for such as should afterward believe on his name, implying that some men would reject him, in consequence of which they must fail of salvation.

5. " Woe unto you, Scribes and Pharisees, hypocrites! for ye shut up the kingdom of heaven against men : for ye neither go in yourselves, neither suffer ye them that are entering to go in." This is another of the numerous proofs of the exclusion of persons in the time of Christ, from the privileges of his kingdom. Enough has been said of the spiritual nature of this kingdom. It was not set up with any temporal design. nor does it secure its subjects from temporal calamities.

John xvii. 9, 20. Math. xxiii. 13.

It is not of this world. It extends beyond the grave, and there, in a peculiar sense, it protects and enriches those, who inherit it, while the servants of sin, are banished and shut up in misery. But the Pharisees entered not into this kingdom, and were accessory to the exclusion of others. Nothing more indubitable is needed in proof of a state of punishment in the future world.

6. " And whosoever shall not receive you, nor hear you, when ye depart thence; shake off the dust under your feet, for a testimony against them. Verily I say unto you, it shall be more tolerable for Sodom and Gomorrah in the day of judgment, than for that city." This passage, which shows that the day of judgment was used technically, for the time when God shall pronounce a final sentence on men of every generation, is of itself sufficient to establish the future punishment of the wicked. The inhabitants of Sodom and Gomorrah are to be called to an account in company with the rejectors of the gospel, who will be most severely punished. " And this is the condemnation, that light has come into the world, and men loved darkness rather than light, because their deeds are evil."

Mark vi. 11. John iii. 19.

It was not the design of Christ's death, to condemn the world, but that the world through him might be saved. But notwithstanding this, the wickedness of man is so great, that he refuses the knowledge which is proffered him, and increases the severity of his doom, by rejecting the means of salvation. In this is plainly implied, not only, that some men will perish, but that the mission of Christ will enhance their condemnation. "But the heavens and the earth, which are now, by the same word are kept in store, reserved unto fire, against the day of judgment and perdition of ungodly men." The import of this cannot be mistaken. We have already noticed the technical meaning of the day of judgment, but here is mentioned the additional circumstance of the general conflagration. The perdition of ungodly men will then take place.

7. " As also in all his epistles, speaking in them of these things; in which are some things hard to be understood, which they that are unlearned and unstable wrest, as they do also the other scriptures, unto their own destruction." The sense in which destruction

2d. Peter, iii. 7, 16.

7

is predicated of the wicked has already been noticed. It is here deserving of more serious consideration, because it is said to follow erroneous views of the bible, which could not be said of any other book, and which on the scheme of universal salvation, is not true. It is only on the supposition, that the scriptures reveal the way in which we must walk or perish, that the distortion of their meaning can involve men in misery.

8. "But after thy hardness and impenitent heart treasurest up unto thyself wrath, against the day of wrath and revelation of the righteous judgment of God. Who will render to every man according to his deeds : to them who by patient continuance in well-doing, seek for glory, and honor, and immortality, eternal life. But unto them that are contentious, and do not obey the truth, but obey unrighteousness, indignation and wrath ; tribulation and anguish, upon every soul of man that doeth evil, of the Jew first and also of the Gentile." This is the last proof passage to be cited on this occasion, and not the least decisive. It evidently relates to the retribu-

Romans ii. 5—9.

tions of eternity. The day of wrath and of the revelation of the righteous judgment of God, properly designates the day of judgment. It is now with God a time of mercy. Nor is there any period of probation, which can be proclaimed to the world as pre-eminently disclosing his indignation and righteous judgments. The punishment is also represented to be the result of an obstinate impenitency, and of a gradual preparation for final condemnation. But what is most convincing, is the opposition, which is presented, between the condition of those who obey not the gospel, and that of the righteous, who by patient continuance in well doing, seek for glory, honor and immortality. To these eternal life is given, while those are recompensed with indignation and wrath, tribulation and anguish. What can more plainly declare the future misery of a portion of mankind? Were I seeking to express the doctrine in terms that defy a false construction, I could not avail myself of better language. Here then I might safely leave my hearers to decide whether future punishment is a doctrine of the bible. Let, however, the following considerations be candidly weighed.

1. *The evidence which has been adduced, though amply sufficient for the purpose, is but a small part of what might be advanced.* I have purposely avoided those passages, which relate to other topics in the general question before us. But even were the texts, hereafter to be noticed, and those already examined, erased from the sacred page, the truth which they assert, would still remain in legible characters. It would be safe to undertake this controversy, were every text which I shall employ in these lectures denied me. And what may seem more surprising to some, it might be sustained by passages, taken exclusively from the epistles of St. Paul.

2. Should it be said, that that branch of the subject, treated of in this and the preceding lectures has commanded an undue share of attention, since most persons admit, that the wicked will suffer, at least for a limited period; it may be replied, that my design embraces not only a collection of the evidence, necessary to establish the doctrine of future punishment, but an elucidation and defence of the passages, which declare it. My hearers must have noticed, that while most universalists admit the doctrine of a limited punishment,

they task themselves, with the labor of deducing a different sense from every passage, which teaches it. Though, however, most of them in our day adopt the notion of a final restoration of the wicked, admitting that they will suffer for a season, yet there are those who contend for the immediate salvation of the whole world. To them the preceding arguments are addressed.

3 *The conclusion to which we have arrived exhibits sin as a very great evil.* How offensive to God is the conduct, which involves men in the miseries of hell, even if those miseries are temporary! That must be more odious and abominable than mankind are apt to allow, which induces a good and merciful Being, to execute on the wicked such a punishment, as indignation and wrath, tribulation and anguish, denote. Weeping, wailing and gnashing of teeth, the smoke of a bottomless pit, the flames of a lake of fire, are terrible descriptions. This life presents no parallel to the pain and agony, here figured forth. But sin is the cause of it. What men often regard of trivial consequence, of casual occurrence, and of indifferent character in the sight of

7 *

God, produces not only mental and bodily anguish here, but more horrid sufferings hereafter. On what principle of prudence then, is sin so often treated as a harmless gaiety or a pardonable weakness. It seems strange, if they believe their own creed, that those who admit the temporary punishment of the wicked, are not startled at this reflected picture of human depravity. But perhaps the spirit of unbelief which causes them to doubt the doctrine of *eternal* punishment, impairs the force of conviction, in respect to a temporary infliction. However this may be, there is no surer inference from our doctrine than the inexpressible odiousness of sin.

4. *Too great efforts and sacrifices to rescue men from perdition, cannot be made.* The alarm of the awakened sinner, the intense anxiety of one pleading for pardon, the urgent entreaties of friends, the affectionate warnings and persuasive eloquence of the pulpit, feebly express the value of the soul. It is a theme, which should engross every mind; it should draw to itself the resources of Christendom, fill the coffers of every evangelical society, send the missionaries of the cross throughout the world, give the bible to every family, re-

form the press, impart to the pulpit new weight and unction, break up every intemperate habit, render solitary every haunt of vice, it should make the world solemn and produce the universal enquiry;—"what shall I do to be saved." All this is true, were the wicked eventually to be reprieved. And is religious solicitude useless and superstitious? Is the believer in eternal punishment the only person, who acts inconsistently, while he lives in the neglect of duty? Is there not something peculiarly astonishing in the well known stupidity of the restorationist? Can he be sincere in professing to believe, that the wicked will suffer for ages the most excruciating torments, and yet manifest such cold indifference to their spiritual welfare? He accuses believers in eternal punishment of insincerity, because their solicitude for the wicked is not always uniform, nor ever adequate to the interest involved. Yet when did *he* ever manifest compassion for those who, according to his own admission, are to perish for ages of ages? But I forbear; so awful a subject must not be treated like a question between man and man. Yet let not Christians be reproached for the anxiety which they do feel and manifest in behalf of the soul, for feelings deeper than other hearts experience, for efforts which afford true religion a place on earth, and which will ultimately extend it throughout the world.

LECTURE IV.

THE GRADATIONS OF FUTURE PUNISHMENT.

━━◖◗━━

LUKE xii. 47, 48.

*And that servant, which knew his Lord's will,
and prepared not himself, neither did according
to his will, shall be beaten with many stripes.
But he that knew not, and did commit things
worthy of stripes, shall be beaten with few
stripes.*

DIVINES have not always been careful to
give a proper representation of the difference,
which the various wickedness of lost men
will occasion, in the intensity of their sufferings. All are described in some sermons, as
sharing equally in the shame and anguish of
despair. The consequence has been an entire denial of the doctrine of future punishment, as too horrible for human belief. The
object of the present lecture is to exhibit the

subject, as far as ability serves me, in its true light, that such unreasonable prejudices may be removed.

God is able to make the conditions of the wicked in the next life, very various, and far more unlike than the extremes of misery endured on earth. In the exercise of this prerogative, He expressly declares, that there shall be an impartial distribution of justice. " Every man shall receive his own reward, according to his own labor." " For we must all appear before the judgment seat of Christ, that every one may receive the things done in his body, *according to that he hath done, whether it be good or bad.*" " But *after* thy hardness and impenitent heart, treasurest up unto thyself, wrath against the day of wrath, and revelation of the righteous judgment of God; who will render to *every man according to his deeds.*" " But I say unto you, that it shall be more tolerable for the land of Sodom in the day of judgment, than for thee." " To whom men have committed much, of him will they ask the more." The text is also explicit on this subject. It is a direct assertion, that those who sin against the clearest light and best opportunities of knowing the divine will, shall be most severely punished. "And that servant which knew his lord's will, and prepared not himself, neither did according to his will, shall be beaten with many stripes. But he that knew not, and did commit things worthy of stripes, shall be beaten with few strips." Such is the evidence, that a gradation will be observed, in the sufferings of the wicked.

Before this truth is presented in its practical bearings, it is important to notice two erroneous theories, which have much influence in forming the views of christians on the general subject. The first of these supposes, that punishment will be proportioned to the capacities of men. The same view is taken by its abettors, in respect to those who are saved. They are said to be, as happy as their capacities admit. All are represented perfectly happy, but not equally so, in consequence of their various capacities for enjoyment. As those who receive the least pleasure are incapable of receiving more, until their powers are enlarged, they can have no ungratified desires, and are therefore completely happy; but the most exalted intelligences are inconceivably happier, because

more exquisitely susceptible. Such in principle. is the theory in respect to those who perish. They are said to suffer as much as possible with existing capacities. but not equally,
nor as much as they will, when their sensibilities become more acute, or when their powers are more expanded. This theory, by ap-
portioning to men suffering in different degrees, only *seems* to be in accordance with the
scriptural account of rewards and punishments; for those who are to be happy or
miserable according to their works, are not
good and bad according to their capacities.
Persons, whose intellectual and moral faculties have been most fully developed and ma-
tured, have not always been most distinguished for piety and good works. According to
the representations of the bible. it is not irra-
tional to expect, that some, who are not far
removed from idiocy, will be more richly rewarded than many, who have been pre-emi-
nent in human and divine knowledge. That
minds, whose capacities for enjoyment are so
far from being exactly measured by their
faith and virtues, will be changed and mould-
ed after death, that they may receive their
just rewards according to this theory, is a

very unphilosophical supposition. But there are objections to its admission, still more decisive. Happiness does not depend upon filling a person's capacity. It might produce satiety, and prevent desire, but could not convey the purest and richest enjoyment. A sense of the desirableness of things as yet unobtained, is not inconsistent with happiness. Such is the nature of the mind, it may be doubted, whether a feeling, that we do not possess all which we wish, is not essential to our enjoying anything. There must be some object of pursuit, something which the mind desires, and which it is conscious of not having, or it is at once cut off from the pleasures of activity and enterprize. The theory is unsound in other respects. What is a capacity for enjoyment, except the power of exercising the faculties on pleasing subjects ? The power of loving must forever be a principal source of gratification. But the heart is always able to love a new and worthy object, without the least alteration in its faculties. We can never say,—its capacities are now full—it can love no more. Two spirits. in the same rank of intelligences, may indeed be contented in the unequal rewards, which God

8

bestows upon them. He may reveal to one, while he conceals from the other, objects, which both might appreciate and enjoy. Thus he may distribute his rewards in various proportions, according to the characters of men of the same powers. But how a capacity for enjoyment can be surfeited, how one can be as happy as possible, I cannot divine. From the nature of the affections, in the exercise of which is our chief enjoyment, we must ever be capable of delighting in a new object of pleasure. How then can our happiness be perfect ? Happy as the case admits, we may be, in consequence of possessing no new sources of pleasure ; when were those sources opened. our satisfaction would be exquisite. We are often as happy as circumstances allow, while other circumstances might make us happier. The same may be said of our offerings. The spirits of lost men may be capable of keener anguish than they will ever experience, and though they should all be equally susceptible, no two might suffer equally. Were their capacities for pain proportional to their guilt, these capacities could not be filled, as the common theory supposes. For the term capacity in this, as in the other case, represents the mind to be something like a measure or resorvoir, into which a definite quantity of misery can be poured. Moral acts, under whatever class they come, are acts of the will, and the fact that the will has acted in reference to ten thousand objects, does not impair its ability of acting, in reference to ten thousand more. Lost spirits hate the perfections of God, and envy the enjoyments of heaven, so far as they are acquainted with them; but a clearer view might, without any alteration in themselves, inflame their passions and embitter their sufferings. So absurd is it, to speak of filling their capacities when every new object presented to their minds, may occasion some tormenting excitement! I have thought it desirable to expose this prevalent opinion, because, while it seems to admit a gradation in future punishment, founded on an impartial distribution of justice, it actually contradicts it by representing men as destined to endure all that is possible with their susceptibilities and powers.

The other theory, connected with this subject, is equally unsupported by the scriptures, though philosophically more plausible. It supposes, that the powers, both of redeemed and lost men, will constantly expand and strengthen, and cause a constant and unlimited progression, in the happiness of the one and in the misery of the other. This is a mere hypothesis. An increase of capacity, does not necessarily imply, an increase of suffering. Though philosophy teaches, that a growing knowledge of facts, may constantly raise the tone of wretchedness, it also proves, that habit may make that tolerable, which once seemed ready to crush the sufferer. Perhaps the wicked will become more and more miserable, and the righteous more and more blessed, but the idea, unsustained by the bible and by reason, is a supposition altogether gratuitous; to which, as well as to the preceding theory, I cannot but object, because, while it serves no valuable purpose, it prejudices the thinking world against the truth.

But dismissing these and other theories, advanced without sufficient support, I invite your attention to the practical views, suggested by the text.

1. *Every thing done on earth in the service of God, will increase the happiness of heaven.* Not one holy feeling or act, not one emotion of love,

of contentment or of submission, not one
prayer of faith, or tear of pity, or deed of self-
denial, or triumph in temptation, shall be un-
rewarded. Such is the doctrine of our Savior;—" And whosoever shall give to drink,
unto one of these little ones, a cup of cold
water only, in the name of a disciple, verily, I
say unto you, he shall in no wise lose his reward" But I introduce it, as an inference
from the text. It is a principle of God's
government, to reward men according to
their deeds, in consistency with the doctrine
of salvation by faith. He bestows his favors
upon those who believe, in proportion to their
fidelity in his service. He takes a just estimate of their characters, by considering the
age in which they lived, the privileges which
they enjoyed, the trials to which they were
exposed, the number and precise nature of all
their volitions, and whatever has served to
make them what they are. With this perfect
knowledge of their moral standing, he assigns
them their seats in paradise. This is a fact of
great practical importance. It speaks in the
language of our Saviour;—" Lay up for yourselves treasures in heaven, where neither

8 *

moth nor rust doth corrupt, and where thieves do not break through and steal." We think it wise, to labor in youth to make manhood respectable, and in manhood to smooth the decline of life; although the child may never see mature years, nor the adult old age; and although, if they do, their efforts may prove abortive, and their hopes be dashed. How much wiser it is, to labor for the meat that never perisheth, for the garments that never decay, for the crown that never fades; how much wiser, to be diligent and active, where every effort is successful, and the success so glorious! Can any subject commend itself more strongly to our love of happiness, or more effectually engage our best thoughts and efforts? Can a christian, whose faith has any strength, hesitate, whether to deny himself for the name of Christ, whether to resist temptation, whether to cultivate his piety, when his reward is so sure and so rich? Is there a man, with views so low, with taste so corrupt, that he will not relinquish momentary and sordid pleasures, that he will not endure the labors of an hour, for pure and lasting enjoyment?

2. *Impenitent men should avoid sin as their worst enemy.* I say not this, on the ground of its tendency to impair the moral and intellectual faculties, and to diminish the prospect of conversion, but as an inference from views, taken in this discourse. I say it, because men are to be rewarded according to their deeds. It is awfully dangerous to sin. Every kind of disobedience will receive a just recompense, every species and degree of iniquity will be punished, every offence will contribute to the misery of the soul. Two spirits may be wretched, both destitute of positive enjoyment, while the condition of one, in comparison with that of the other, is almost beatitude. This should have a mighty influence on the public morals. It should give sanctity to the civil oath, it should purify human affections, it should regulate all the affairs of life. In every conceivable case, it is adapted to awaken salutary fears. What can be presented to a reflecting mind, more weighty than that which connects sin with certain and exemplary punishment? When the consequences of a single offence are tremendous, shall we multiply our crimes? Shall we, reckless of results, rush on the bosses of the

Almighty's buckler? Yet there are men who disregarding the consequences of individual sins, boast of obtaining happiness by unlawful means, on as large a scale as possible. Such are they especially, who, in consequence of the inveteracy of vicious propensities, despair of reformation. Looking at heaven, as above their attainment, and at hell as their destined home, they resolve to indulge themselves to the utmost. They appear not to dream, that God will call them into judgment, for every offence. They think not in what rank of sufferers they are to be classed. Their folly is like his, who should take on himself the worst evils of life, because he cannot escape the least. Though this persuasion of the hopelessness of their condition were well founded, how wise it would be, to shun every sin. If they are to perish, they should shrink from vice in its least degree and mildest form, as the envenomer of every bitter feeling, and as an auxiliary to every foe of the soul, that will meet it down the track of eternity. With how many agonizing recollections, with how many stings of conscience, with how many dismal anticipations, with how many stripes from indignant justice, will one sin besiege the imprisoned spirit forever! And who, in view of this impending storm, will come out in provocation? The sinner challenges the wrath of God. Were it not ourselves, who are thus presumptuous, sin would appear the extreme of madness, as well as of guilt. Oh let us never forget, that the misery of lost souls will be measured by the number and character of their transgressions! If we are in wicked habits, or exposed to peculiar temptations, let us learn the invaluable importance of reformation and of moral resistance. Let us learn the motives, which exist, not only for christians to be eminently holy, but for all men, to be scrupulously virtuous.

It has been the design of the preceding remarks, to fasten on the mind, both how much the joys of heaven depend on vigilance in the divine life, and how much the sufferings of hell owe their edge and weight, to looseness of morals. Unhappy you may be, in despite of all which mercy can devise to save you, yet not so unhappy as you are in danger of becoming. It is one thing to perish, and quite another thing to perish, an old, hardened and abandoned transgressor; it is one thing for a heathen to be condemned, and quite another thing to perish from a land of b.b.es and of sabbaths : it is a glorious thing to be saved at all, but unspeakably more so, to be saved as an apostle.

3. Since the retributions of eternity are dispensed unequally to those whose capacities are nearly the same, it is evident, that the redeemed are less happy, and that those who perish are less miserable, than their powers admit. It may, however, be proper to say, in popular language, that all the inhabitants of heaven are perfectly happy. Who is not convinced, that a sight of the superior enjoyments of apostles and prophets, and holy martyrs of the cross, exalted above others in the heavenly world, can cause no diminution of happiness, to inferior saints? Those whose rewards are the least, are still the children of God, and have the spirit of Christ. They are thankful for what they receive, and envy not those, who receive more. They must, notwithstanding, be sensible of their inferiority. Their views are not so clear, nor so various, nor is their condition so exalted. as appertains to those, who served God better in this life. They feel, that they are capable of higher happiness, they perceive such happiness is

desirable; and they can only be called perfectly happy, inasmuch as their feelings are all holy, and their enjoyments very great, while not a shadow of positive evil, is allowed to approach them. And though the wicked do not suffer, as severely as possible, they may be said, in popular language, to be perfectly miserable. Some drink deeper of the cup of trembling, than others in the same rank of intelligence, but as they are all unholy, and all tormented, without the least alleviation, they may be called perfectly wretched.

4. *The views which have been taken do not diminish the dread, which the world of woe should inspire.* Its mildest forms of suffering, may transcend our present feeble conceptions. The language in which it is described, conveys to the mind, a picture of misery, beyond any thing endured in this world. Those terrific names of the mansions of despair, hell, hell-fire, the furnace of fire, the fire which is never quenched, outer darkness, weeping and gnashing of teeth, imply a great degree of severity in every case of punishment. There will be no injustice. None will suffer more than he deserves, and every man as much. Yet the lowest seat in heaven, is an archan-

gelic condition, compared with that of the least sufferer in hell. To be saved is one thing, to perish is another, infinitely unlike and unutterably worse. In destruction, is involved the loss of all good and the sufferance of all the evil, which those names of horrid import describe. In attempting to set this doctrine in its true light, and to remove the objections, which indiscriminate views and unfounded hypotheses, have raised, I have not robbed it of practical force. It still appears dreadful to perish. Who can number his own sins? Who can tell, to what class of sinners he belongs? We have then every motive, to escape that unknown condition of wretchedness, to which we are exposed. Nor would it contribute to any good practice, to imagine, that the redeemed are equally happy. It is the gracious purpose of God, to reward the penitent according to their services, and to punish the wicked according to their sins. In this, there is much to excite to virtue, much to deter from sin. Does man reflect on this, when he indulges his favorite vice? When envy, breeding hatred and discontent, is harbored in his bosom, does he remember, that God will bring him into

judgment? When avarice, making him unjust, penurious, oppressive and fraudulent,
obtains possession of his heart, does he remember, that God will bring him into judgment? When the love of applause, subjecting virtue, consistency, honor and religion to
disgrace, usurps his mind, does he remember,
that God will bring him into judgment? When
ambition, darkening his reason, his principles
and his practice, becomes his passion, does he
remember, that God will bring him into judgment? When pleasure, weakening his in-
tellect, contracting his views, degrading his
taste, and impairing his usefulness, gains the
ascendant, does he remember, that God will
bring him into judgment? When intemperance, inflaming his appetite, depriving him of
conscience, ruining his family, disgracing and
corrupting his species, dishonoring his God
and brutalizing his own soul, seizes him for
its slave, does he remember that God will
bring him into judgment? When stubborn
unbelief, chilling the best sensibilities of the
heart, disabling the best faculties of the mind,
and shutting down on the soul the doors of
darkness, asserts its undisputed authority over
him, does he remember, that God will bring

him into judgment ? No ;—could he constantly behold, how the flames of his future dwelling brighten up with more fervid heat and
horrid glare on every new act of disobedience,
it would destroy his unlawful pleasures. The
laughter of sin is thoughtless. It is only
when God is forgotten, or his word uncredited,
that iniquity is pleasant. Let the heart, then,
prompt the memory, and the memory remind
the heart, that for every secret thing God will
bring thee into judgment—that for every new
act of rebellion, justice will demand reprisal.

LECTURE V.

THE DURATION OF FUTURE PUNISHMENT.

MARK ix. 47, 48.

And if thine eye offend thee, pluck it out : it is better for thee, to enter into the kingdom of God with one eye, than having two eyes to be cast into hell-fire ; where their worm dieth not, and the fire is not quenched.

THE present lecture is devoted to the question at issue between believers in eternal punishment, and those who expect the restoration of the wicked to virtue and happiness. They admit, that a part of mankind will be condemned to a place of torment. but suppose that there is a limit to their sufferings, that in the progress of ages the period will arrive, when having repented, or having expiated their crimes by an adequate punishment, they will be restored to divine favor. i cannot subscribe to their opinion. The bible is full and explicit in declaring, that the state of the wicked in another world is unalterably fixed. Before the proof of this is presented, it is desirable to notice several things, which are often overlooked in the controversy.

1. *The supposition, that the wicked. when once condemned, will ever be reprieved, is altogether gratuitous.* All the passages, which speak of their punishment, leave the question of its duration untouched, or represent it to be eternal. Nothing is implied in them, like the doctrine of restoration. They either assert, that all men are saved on the same terms and at the same time, or they do not teach universal salvation in any form. It cannot, therefore, be pretended, that the views, which we are opposing. have any support in the sacred scriptures. It is true, that formerly a passage in the third chapter of the Acts of the apostles, and another in the first Epistle of Peter, were mentioned as favoring such a supposition, but the idea is now generally abandoned. It certainly cannot be sustained. In one of these, it is declared, that heaven must receive the Lord Jesus Christ until the restitution of all things, which God hath spoken by the mouth of all his holy prophets. since the world

began. But it is now admitted, that this restitution, signifies the final accomplishment of the divine predictions. When, whatever has been foretold by the prophets is fulfilled, the Lord will make his second advent and close up the history of this world. In the other passage, it has been supposed, that the apostle spake of our Lord's visiting the abodes of the damned, and proclaiming to them the offers of salvation. "By which also he went and preached to the spirits in prison, which sometime were disobedient, when once the long suffering of God, waited in the days of Noah, while the ark was a preparing, wherein few, that is. eight souls, were saved by water." By joining this with the preceding verse, and observing the sense of each part, this only will appear to be taught, that Christ, who existed in his spiritual nature in the time of Noah, went in that nature and preached unto the antediluvians, who then lived, but are now in prison. *For Christ hath once suffered for sins, the just for the unjust, that he might bring us to God, being put to death in the flesh, (that is as respects his human nature) but quickened by the spirit (that is, as respects his spiritual nature) in which spiritual nature he also*

9 *

went and preached to the spirits now in prison,
who aforetime in the days of Noah were disobedi-
ent. But it is not important, that I should in-
sist upon a point, which probably none will
dispute. The doctrine of restoration, is not
taught in the bible. Were it therefore true,
that all the passages relating to future punishment, leave its duration unascertained,
would it not be presumptuous, to risk the
soul on the uncertain supposition of its becoming in the lapse of ages, holy and happy?
Let the following be assumed, as an example
of all that God has said on the subject;—
" And now also the axe is laid unto the root
of the trees : therefore, every tree that bring-
eth not forth good fruit, is hewn down and
cast into the fire." " Brethren if any of you
do err from the truth, and one convert him;
let him know, that he which converteth the
sinner from the error of his way, shall save a
soul from death, and shall hide a multitude of
sins." Here the certainty of punishment is
asserted, but not its endless duration. Yet,
if there is no intimation in the bible, that it
will ever cease, is it not hazardous to conclude, that it will? This state of the question,
I fear, is often disregarded ; and men heed-

lessly set themselves to prove, that everlasting is not eternal, imagining that if this can be done, they need entertain no apprehension of endless condemnation. But were it only declared in the bible that the wicked shall be punished, while the righteous are made happy, it would involve a fearful probability, that they will never meet again.

2. *Were the doctrine of restoration true, it would probably have been taught by Christ.* This, believers in it must admit, because they always describe it as a supposition most glorious to God and as absolutely essential to the vindication of his character. They should, therefore, sustain their views by direct and unequivocal testimony from the scriptures. Unless such testimony can be produced, their opinions must be considered unworthy of confidence; especially since the greatest interests are involved in arriving at a correct conclusion. To this reason for expecting an explicit declaration of the final restoration of the wicked, provided it is to take place, may be added, *the integrity of the divine government.* It cannot be imagined, that God would systematically employ error, in controlling and actuating his creatures. Either by direct

testimony from Him, or by the want of contrary testimony, the doctrine of eternal punishment has gained the almost undivided conviction of mankind. It has been believed by millions, in every age, and has had a forming hand in their lines of conduct and feeling. Is this a superstition? Can it be supposed, that God has left a being so imaginative as man, to shudder at ideal forms of distress, and to array with withering apprehensions, a doctrine, which teaches nothing but fatherly corrections or momentary reproof? Let it not be forgotten, that one text. well authenticated, declaring that the wicked shall suffer only for a season, would have effectually excluded the doctrine of eternal punishment from the christian creed. But there nevertheless it stands, and influences unnumbered minds; it alarms, it convicts, it urges men to let go of earth, to dash down the cup of iniquity, to press into life. It must be recollected too, that human predilections are not in its favor. Men have been led to believe, in despite of their wishes. It has had opposers; it has been hated, defamed, persecuted from city to city, and handed about with hissing and invective. Still, the body of those who call themselves christians, confess, that it is taught in their scriptures, and that they can discover no appearances of a contrary doctrine. This could scarcely be the case, were a final restoration spoken of in the bible. Indeed, it is inconsistent with such an idea, for it cannot reasonably be admitted, that God would conceal the truth, for the sake of influencing men by fears of imaginary evil. He would not prevail on them to obey him, by permitting them to apprehend a fate, infinitely more dreadful than the worst beings will ever endure. If then the doctrine of restoration is true, whence arises the silence of the scriptures concerning it? a silence, from which, if not from more direct testimony, has resulted the almost universal persuasion, that the torments of hell will never end.

3. *The first hearers of the gospel must have understood future punishment to be eternal, unless the contrary was expressly affirmed by their teachers.* The Jews, in the time of our Savior, believed, that all, who were not embraced in the covenant made with Abraham, would perish forever. Every scholar also knows, that eternal punishment was a favorite theme of the Greek and Latin poets, and a popular

notion of the multitude. When, therefore, Christ and his apostles came to speak of the place of torment, their hearers, whether Jews or Pagans, would need to have their opinions, if erroneous, corrected. If nothing was said on the subject, and no intimation given that they were in an error, they would naturally conclude, that they had not been mistaken, and would continue to believe in eternal punishment. It hence, most manifestly devolves upon believers in a final restoration, to show in what place and in what manner, Christ and his apostles ever controverted the popular opinion.

4. *That the wicked will never be restored to virtue and happiness, is fairly inferred from the moral tendency of punishment.* Alone it can never produce contrition. The first inducement to repent, which can operate on the human mind, is the apprehension of personal evil. But neither that apprehension, nor actual suffering, can subdue the will and melt the heart. Danger may excite alarm and induce inquiry, but it cannot reconcile a rebellious mind and call forth emotions of gratitude and love. The goodness of God leadeth men to repentance. It is not the fire of hell, which

can make them sorry after a godly sort. That can only add intensity to their hate, and inflame their malevolence against God and his laws. It is not in the nature of man, to be thus won to holy views and feelings. The infliction of punishment, therefore, supplies no means and affords no prospect, of the voluntary subjection of the wicked to the government of God. It rather, by exciting opposition, and confirming hatred, tends to perpetuate rebellion.

5. *If the wicked deserve any punishment, as its infliction proves they do, they will never cease to deserve it.* They take very partial views of the subject, who imagine, that the sins of this life are the only actions, for which the final rejectors of the gospel will be confined in despair. They will increase their own ill desert, by ceaseless resistance to the government of God. The sins done in the body do indeed merit everlasting destruction. But were this denied, the wicked in hell are perpetually violating the unimpaired obligation of supreme love to God, and consequently creating a reason for their endless punishment. Did not the nature of the case establish this, the word of God would make it certain.

" Let him that is filthy be filthy still." Moral impurity consists in a bad state of the affections. Were the wicked to exercise pious feelings, they would no longer be unclean. They will, it hence appears, continue in sin. In other words, the souls of lost men are under a law, which they violate, and to the penalties of which, they are unceasingly exposing themselves. The time can never arrive, in which they will not deserve additional punishment for acts just committed. While they are suffering for the sins of this life, they will be provoking the justice of God to punish them for new, more numerous and it may be more aggravated offences. The sin of the fallen angels, in tempting our first parents to take the forbidden fruit and in deceiving their posterity, is no more punishable than the sins, which wicked men will commit after their final sentence. And as both the bible and the nature of the case show, that they will continue to offend, there is a reason constantly arising, for perpetuating their punishment.

6. *If the doctrine of restoration is true, the wicked will be released without deserving acquittal, or they will escape, having expiated their sins by an adequate punishment, on the ground of justice.*

But it is not pretended, from any thing in the bible, that they will ever be restored because they no longer deserve to be punished. Such a supposition is often made, but it is not found in the word of God. The salvation of men, as far as it extends, is always spoken of as the result of forgiveness. The texts, which are employed to prove universal salvation refer the whole effect, whatever it is, to the mercy of God; and in no instance intimate that the wicked will expiate their sins and complete the period of lawful punishment, by suffering to the extent of their crimes. None of these imply the doctrine of restoration on the ground of justice, whatever else they may teach. If, as it is alleged, they assert it at all, it is through the mediation of Christ and the forgiveness of sins. But lost men will not escape through forgiveness, for the scriptures are most explicit in deciding that there is no pardon beyond the grave. " But if ye forgive not men their trespasses, neither will your father forgive your trespasses." The doctrine of restoration is, therefore, not true, because neither of the suppositions on which it rests, can be maintained.

7. *The above conclusion is, with equal satis-*

faction, *established by many of the passages, which have been quoted to prove merely that there is a state of future punishment.* In them it is declared, that certain men shall not inherit the kingdom of God, that they shall in no case enter into it, that they shall have their portion in the world of misery. These denunciations leave no room for an honest doubt, that their sufferings will be perpetual. Were the scriptures silent, as it respects a more clear and positive declaration on the subject, it might justly be thought hazardous to deny the eternity of future punishment.

These considerations, I present to my hearers, not as unanswerable arguments; though, taken collectively, they are enough to convince me of the unreasonableness and temerity of expecting deliverance from the world of despair. The sources of evidence, to which I hereafter call your attention, afford such as is explicit and unanswerable.

1. *The curse of the law, or the penalty by which it is enforced, is eternal death.* That from which men are rescued by faith in Jesus Christ, is that to which they expose themselves by sin. "And as Moses lifted up the serpent in the wilderness, even so must the Son of Man be

lifted up, that whosoever believeth in him should not *perish*, but have *eternal life.* For God so loved the world. that he gave his only begotten Son, that whosoever believeth in him should not perish, but have *everlasting life.*" Christ came to save men from destruction, and to confer on them eternal happiness. But if they, by violating the law, have not forfeited this happiness. it cannot be the design of christianity to confer it. Without a Savior, they are condemned. in consequence of their sins, to eternal exclusion from heaven; and as perishing is the antithesis of this, to eternal suffering. Such happiness Christ confers, such misery he averts; and hence it follows, that the curse of the law, or that which is incurred by transgression, is endless punishment. But those. who reject the gospel, which we have seen some men do, incur this penalty, and can, therefore, on the ground of justice, never escape. It is to be observed, too, that as believers are saved by faith, as the only condition of salvation. it implies, that the consequences of unbelief are eternal. Why should everlasting life be promised them, as a reward of repentance and faith, if they have not forfeited it, and if they are, whatever their conduct may be, to enjoy it? Christ would not, in such a case, be the author of eternal life. but only a Savior from temporary evils, and the author of happiness, during that limited period.

II. *The text and other passages of similar phraseology, are unequivocal evidence against the doctrine of restoration.* They declare that the wicked shall be punished with unquenchable fire. or that there shall be no termination to their torments. "Whose fan is in his hand, and he will thoroughly purge his floor, and will gather the wheat into his garner, but the chaff he will burn with fire unquenchable." "And if thy hand offend thee, cut it off: it is better for thee to enter into life maimed, than having two hands to go into hell, into the fire that never shall be quenched: where their worm dieth not, and the fire is not quenched." These declarations will receive a separate and particular examination. It is important, however, to make my younger hearers first acquainted with a rule of interpretation, to be applied in the subsequent part of this discourse and of essential use in decipher-

Luke 3. 19.   Mark 9. 43. 44

ing the meaning of language. The rule is
this. *Words are to be used in their common and
obvious import, unless it is modified by the nature
of the subject or by the design of the writer.*
Universal terms, as the world, mankind,
all men, are sometimes to be limited, but
never, unless the context makes it apparent,
that the whole human race is not intended.
It thus happens, also, that terms expressing
duration denote the longest period of which
the subject united with them, is capable. The
same word may, in one application, express
an absolute eternity, while in another it includes only a short period of time. But no
ambiguity, or perplexity arises from this various use of language, because the subject itself
always announces its exact signification.
You sell an estate, assigning it to the pur-
chaser and his heirs *forever*, and though forever in its common sense expresses an absolute eternity, it is not in this connexion thus
understood. If you should speak of losing
your soul forever, the language would be
equally intelligible. In the first instance,
forever signifies the longest period in which
an estate can be entailed, or until it shall be
voluntarily disposed of; and in the other case.

10 *

it signifies the longest period, in which the soul can be lost. Let this rule be applied, and no doubt will exist, whether the duration spoken of is limited or not. When that which is said to be eternal, without end, unquenchable, or forever, is something which belongs exclusively to time, it limits the signification of these terms. But when it is something, which in its nature extends beyond the grave, and may subsist without end, these terms are not to be limited, but to be taken in their literal sense, as denoting an absolute eternity. The everlasting hills or mountains, are hills or mountains, which remain as long as time endures. The subject, of which everlasting is here predicated, does not admit of a longer duration than the continuance of the earth. The everlasting God is a being, whose existence is not bounded by time. In the first of these instances, everlasting denotes a temporary, but in the second, an endless duration. It may be said of the fire of a perpetually active volcano, that it is unquenchable, that it never shall be quenched, without causing any misapprehension or leading the hearer to suppose, that his informant believes the earth shall never be destroyed. And the language might be true, under the limitation which the subject imposes. When it is said also of the fire of hell, that it is unquenchable, that it never shall be quenched, the declaration is equally unambiguous; for as the subject is not limited by the boundaries of time, it is capable of an absolute eternity. It is satisfactorily inferred, that the fires of hell shall never be quenched, or never cease to burn; or, by stripping the idea of its figurative dress, that the miseries of lost men will never terminate. It is, therefore, scarcely necessary, when we examine these passages by just principles of interpretation, to give them any further notice. It is enough to assert, without other proof, that they teach the endless duration of future torments. For such an assertion cannot be disproved. Instances may perhaps be cited, in which unquenchable is applied to punishments which have an end, but never in any case where future punishment is the subject of affirmation. Temporal calamities may be described, under the figure of unquenchable fire, provided they continue so long as the subjects of them exist, but the punishments of the future world cannot be thus described, unless they are absolutely endless. Allow me to comprehend what has been said in one sentence. If God threatens a nation with his displeasure, declaring that his wrath shall burn and none shall quench it, it is understood, that this nation shall be involved in calamities as long as it endures, but if he threatens persons in reference to the future state with indignation, which shall burn and not be quenched, it can only denote an endless punishment. It may be remarked, too, that as God never threatens men with temporal calamities, in language of such severe reprobation, unless they are very abandoned sinners, it may be used, even in such cases, with reference to punishments which shall succeed this life and be literally perpetual. In illustration of these facts, nothing better could be desired, than the passages so often quoted from the Old Testament to show, that the terms everlasting and unquenchable, when applied to the miseries of the damned, do not denote eternal punishment.— " It shall not be quenched night nor day; the smoke thereof shall go up forever, from generation to generation it shall lie waste; none shall pass through it forever and ever." " Behold, mine anger and my fury shall be poured out upon this place, upon man and upon beast, and upon the trees of the field, and upon the fruit of the ground; and it shall burn and shall not be quenched." " And I will bring an everlasting reproach upon you, and a perpetual shame, which shall not be forgotten." There is no misunderstanding these passages. They apply the words, everlasting, unquenchable, forever and ever, to judgments which were to fall, in part at least upon the wicked in this life. and which were utterly to ruin them. The hopelessness of their condition, the inflexible purpose of God, never to forgive. and never to withdraw his hand from the work of destruction. is thus forcibly expressed. No one is in danger of supposing, that an absolute eternity is intended, so far as the subject of discourse is, in its own nature, temporary. The smoke of the land of Idumea, cannot literally ascend up forever and ever. The reader very properly limits the language, to mean, that it will be an object of the divine displeasure. so long as it exists. But this denunciation, as well as that of bringing upon the Jews an everlasting reproach. may relate, not only to temporal calamities, but to the eternal displeasure of God.

Nor does such a supposition, assign a double sense to the language. It only asserts, that God will never be reconciled to those, against whom these threatenings are uttered. And if this is true, if those, whom he pursues with his displeasure to the end of life, are also the enemies of his government, and the objects of his indignation after death, the literal import belongs to the language. But however this may be, there is manifestly no argument to be drawn from the Old Testament use of unquenchable and everlasting, against the sense which is generally assigned them in the New. If it should be contended, that the judgments mentioned in the Old Testament, as everlasting and unquenchable, are evidently temporal; then, by a plain rule of interpretation, they are said to last only during the natural lives of those who suffer them ; but if these judgments are of a nature to last forever, everlasting and unquenchable imply that they shall be endless Thus, a case scarcely arises, in which the use of these and similar terms is ambiguous. The words are perpetually used in English books, sometimes denoting an absolute eternity, and sometimes but a short period, yet always with perfect perspicuity.

When some hated truth is not to be rejected, men apply the rule, which has been stated, without knowing it, and arrive at the true sense without failure, and without difficulty. A servant forever, they see at once, is a servant as long as he can be, or during his natural life. To be in heaven forever, is to be there always. But mention those passages, where future punishment is said to be everlasting or unquenchable, and instead of inferring, as they should, that it is endless, they abandon their rule, deny the only just conclusion, and attempt to justify themselves by saying, that everlasting and unquenchable do not always denote an endless duration! A servant forever, they very gravely tell us, is a servant only so long as he lives, and everlasting hills, are hills which endure only while the earth exists! But if they would judge of the meaning of language, when applied to future torments, by the same rule of interpretation, by which they conclude that the righteous shall never lose their seats in heaven, there would not be an universalist among believers in the bible. To say, that the wicked shall be cast into hell, into the fire that never shall be quenched, is to assert, that a punishment, which, in its nature is capable of endless in-fliction, shall never cease. It therefore never will. Were the principle denied on which this conclusion rests, language must in a measure cease to be a medium of thought. How does this audience know, that the speaker is a believer in eternal punishment? He has used terms, no more unambiguous than the sacred writers employ. But you judge of his meaning, by the same rules, which, when applied to their language, would lead you to acknowledge, that future punishment is taught by them. Should you refuse to admit the authority of this rule of interpretation, in cases where future punishment is the subject, you would make its endless duration difficult or impossible to reveal. You can at least imagine that it is eternal, and that God intends to make it known. But what terms, sufficiently explicit, can he employ? If he represents it, under the figure of a fire eternal and unquench-able, you reply, that temporal judgments are sometimes thus described. If you will trifle so egregiously with the plainest rules of criticism, with rules, which, in all other cases, lead you infallibly to correct conclusions, no revelation on the subject can be made you.

By voluntarily abandoning the only safe guide, you lose your way and stumble at every step. The word of God can afford you no light, you wrest it to your own destruction. But though it is true that just rules of interpretation decide, that eternal punishment is taught under the figure of unquenchable fire, yet a particular examination of the passages where the expression occurs, will strengthen the conclusion. To this, your attention is invited. In the third chapter of Matthew, John the Baptist describes the Messiah in these terms. " Whose fan is in his hand, and he will thoroughly purge his floor, and gather his wheat into the garner; but he will burn up the chaff with unquenchable fire." It will not be disputed, that good men are denoted by the wheat, and bad men by the chaff. Christ will gather his wheat into the garner, that is, preserve the righteous from being lost and destroyed; but he will burn up the chaff with unquenchable fire or subject the wicked to ceaseless and everlasting misery. This is the obvious and incontrovertible sense. For when it is recollected, that fire is emblematical of punishment, unquenchable can only signify its endless perpetuity. It is in vain to say, that the fire may be endless, while beings subjected to its action escape. Believers in a restoration assume for granted, that a material fire is meant, which they contend may continue forever while its miserable victims are reprieved. But the language is figurative, being only a forcible mode of expressing the severity of punishment. What then is the use of the adjective unquenchable ? It doubtless has a significant import. As the punishment of which it is descriptive, is manifestly to be inflicted after death, it must denote its endless duration. It cannot mean that the wicked shall be utterly consumed or annihilated, for then to be burned up with fire would convey the whole idea ; unquenchable would be redundant. But the greatest reliance for the illustration of this language, is placed upon the passages in the ninth chapter of Mark, one of which stands at the head of this discourse. It has already been shown, that gehenna, translated hell, is the name of the place of future torment. The fire, which is mentioned in the text, as never to be quenched, denotes the punishments of that world. They never terminate. The fire shall never be quenched. Nor should the other description, contained in the text, be overlooked. "It is better for thee to enter into the kingdom of God with one eye, than having two eyes to be cast into hell-fire, *where their worm dieth not.*" This last expression is likewise borrowed from the valley of Hinnom. There worms preyed on the bodies of the dead, so long as they remained, but when they were enterely decayed, the worms also perished. But it is not so in hell. Worms shall prey on the indestructible forms of the wicked forever, that is, their punishment shall never terminate. Let it not be forgotten in these inquiries, that the worm which dieth not is a figurative representation, and not a philosophical account of future misery. Dead bodies, when thrown out to putrify and decay, present a woful picture of wretchedness and are so far a striking description of the miseries of hell. But there is an obvious point of dissimilarity, to which the text has reference. In one case, the body returns to its native dust and the worm dies; in the other, the body is immortal and the worm which preys on it, never dies. Since the worm denotes the wretched condition of the wicked, its deathless nature signifies that their misery is endless. Nor is this conclusion removed, by the passage in the sixty-sixth chapter of Isaiah, to which Christ seems to have alluded. " And they shall go forth and look upon the carcasses of the men, that have transgressed against me : for their worm shall not die, neither shall their fire be quenched; and they shall be an abhorring unto all flesh." This is said to take place after the conversion of the world, and appears to be a dramatic representation of the glorious state of the church, when it shall be universal, and when all the enemies of God shall be punished. The worm that never dies, the fire that shall never be quenched, are *there* also used to denote the everlasting misery of transgressors.

The remainder of this investigation must be deferred until another opportunity. Believing, however, that the doctrine of eternal punishment is already completely established, I would add a word on the benevolence manifested by a faithful minister of Christ in the discharge of this part of his commission. It is sometimes thought, that they alone imitate the spirit of our divine master, who conceal from their hearers the awful retributions of eternity. But how different is the fact? What compassion is there in concealing evils, to which men are actually exposed and from which they cannot escape, except by efforts specially directed to that end? The dangers which threaten them cannot be avoided, except through faith in Jesus Christ; but this they will never exercise, until the law of God with its terrible sanctions, has been exhibited. The object of preaching is to restore to loyalty the revolted subjects of God by leading them to repentance; which cannot be done where a knowledge of eternal punishment, the only proper measure of guilt is withheld and where a false estimate of character is necessarily made. "They that be whole need not a physician, but they that are sick." Christ is nothing to those, who perceive not the sinfulness of sin nor their own guilt, nor the imminent wrath of God. To such he is no shield nor high tower nor rock of defence nor ark of safety. While they deny that the bible sentences to remediless ruin the impenitent world, they act agreeably to their creed and stand exposed to the gathering storm, till bursting forth, it overwhelms them. How can he, who is ignorant of the sanctions of the law, be convinced of the misery of a wicked state, and of the peculiar glory of those who have their fruit unto holiness? How can he know the odiousness of sin, how can he have a just sense of his unworthiness, how can he exalt the Savior to the first place in his affections, how can he be rescued from his apostacy and from the misery naturally incident to transgression? Such effects belong exclusively to that law which converts the soul, which saves moral beings by fear, which persuades the holy to remain allegiant and the rebellious to return to God. and which thus forms the ground and pillar of the divine government. Grateful indeed should we be, that our danger and way of escape are revealed! We should hear with deep solemnity those truths repeated from the pulpit, upon the belief of which depend the structure of religion in our souls and all our well grounded hopes of a blessed hereafter. Could concealment, on the part of the preacher, render the danger any less real and appalling to his hearers, could he, by persuading them, that God will not punish the wicked, reverse the fact, he would have the semblance of an apology for proclaiming impunity in sin. But he cannot. While, therefore, it remains true, that the wicked shall be turned into hell and all the nations that forget God, it will be benevolent to warn every man of his exposure and to persuade every man by these terrors of the Lord, to renounce his sins and to attach himself to the cross of Christ.

LECTURE VI.

THE DURATION OF FUTURE PUNISHMENT.

—◦◦◦—

2. Peter ii. 17.

These are wells without water, clouds that are carried with a tempest; to whom the mist of darkness is reserved forever.

That lost men will never be restored to happiness is apparent from passages which declare their punishment *to be forever, forever and ever, eternal and everlasting.* The corresponding words in the original Greek, are *aion* and *aionios.* It will be best to acquaint ourselves with their general use and import, before we examine their particular application to future punishment.

I. *Aion* occurs in one hundred and four passages in the New Testament. Of these instances of its use, fifty-nine relate to God or to his kingdom, in such a manner that an absolute eternity must be intended. In six of the remaining passages, it is applied to future punishment. There are only thirty-nine, in which it can be pretended, without begging the question, that it signifies a limited duration. If then, the most common use of the word is to decide its meaning when applied to future punishment, that punishment is proved to be eternal. But a just estimation of the argument to be derived from the applications of this word, depends upon understanding a peculiar sense in which the Jews were accustomed to employ it. They divided duration into two periods. The former comprehended the time anterior to the establishment of the Messiah's kingdom, the latter embraced all succeeding ages. The first of these periods, called the *present aion*, was distinguished by weakness, vice and misery; the second, called the *aion to come*, they supposed, would be a time of uncommon prosperity and peace. In one or the other of these senses, it is used in nearly all the thirty-nine passages mentioned above. The following are fair examples. " But he shall receive an hundred fold, now in this time, houses and brethren and sisters and mothers and children and lands with persecutions; and in the world to come, (the aion to come) eternal life." " Who shall receive manifold more in the present time, and in the world to come, (that age which succeeds the judgment) life everlasting." " The enemy that sowed them is the devil, the harvest is the end of the world, (of the present aion) and the reapers are the angels." " For Demas hath forsaken me, having loved this present world," or the vain and transitory things of the aion which precedes the judgment day and the complete establishment of the Messiah's kingdom. " Now all these things happened unto them for examples, and they are written for our admonition, upon whom the ends of the world, (of this aion or order of things) are come."

It is natural and important to inquire, how the Jews came to attach this signification to a word, which properly denotes unlimited duration. The answer is easy. By dividing duration into two periods, calling one the present age and the other the age to come, they do not necessarily restrict either to the limitations of measurable time. The former age comprehends the present with all past periods, the latter age extends through all which are to come. One extends from everlasting, the other to everlasting—each is a proper eternity. As, however, *aion* is the name of periods antecedent to the happy reign of the Messiah, it often assumes a more limited sense, being sometimes employed without reference to the successions of time for the things of this world, and sometimes for the period of human life. When this use of the word and its origin are considered, it appears that the exceptions to its literal import are very rare. In the instances cited above of its limited signification and in every other in which duration is expressed, it might be translated *eternity*. " Who shall not receive manifold more in the present time, and in the world to come (in the eternity to come) life everlasting." Here, then, I may again demand, if the common use of a word is to decide its meaning in its particular applications, whether eternal punishment is not taught in the following and similar passages. " These are wells without water, clouds that are carried with a tempest, to whom the mist of darkness is reserved *forever*." The evidence on which the question is to be decided, is this;—*Aion* is used two or three times for the universe and several times for the things of this world. In these cases it does not express duration, either limited or eternal, and consequently does not assist us in determining its meaning when it relates to time. In several instances, it either denotes the periods which precede the establishment of the Messiah's kingdom or those which succeed, both of which extend through immeasurable or eternal duration. In all the remaining instances of its use, except six in which it is applied to future punishment, it relates to things which by the admission of all christians are endless. According to its common acceptation, therefore, it is to be translated forever and so understood when future punishment is the subject of affirmation. To this convincing view of the subject an additional consideration is to be added; for the case has not been stated in terms so favorable to the doctrine of eternal punishment as it should be. Whenever *aion* has reference to future punishment, it is put in the accusative case and governed by a preposition signifying " *to.*" In such places, it is necessarily translated, to eternity or forever. Fifty-nine of these are undoubted instances of an endless sense, and the remaining six relate to future punishment, which, so far as common use is concerned, is proof that they too denote eternal duration. Such is the state of the argument in favor of eternal punishment, from the general use of aion. An examination of the passages, in which it occurs, shall now be attempted, for the purpose of showing that there is no occasion for assigning it a meaning foreign to its original and common import. One of these passages has just been quoted and needs no comment. The second, you will find in the epistle of Jude. " Raging waves of the sea, foaming out their own shame, wandering stars, to whom is reserved the blackness of darkness *forever*." This is said of false professors, men of very flagitious lives, who crept into the primitive church and became the authors of great abuses. It is undeniable from the nature of the imagery employed, that their utter and remediless ruin is predicted. The passages next to be cited are in the fourteenth, nineteenth and twentieth chapters of the Apocalypse of St. John. " And the smoke of their torment ascendeth up *forever and ever :* and they have no rest day nor night, who worship the beast and his image and whosoever receiveth the mark of his name." " And again they said, Alleluia !

And her smoke rose up *forever and ever.*" "And the devil that deceived them was cast into the lake of fire and brimstone, where the beast and the false prophet are, and shall be tormented day and night *forever and ever.*" In the first instance, the denunciation is directed against pagan Rome, and the fate of those idolaters is contrasted with the rewards of constancy, which the worshippers of the true God receive in heaven. They are represented as suffering forever in hell, or as destined to suffer through the eternal age which is to come. The second passage describes in the same terms the fate of the unbelieving Jews. In the last, it is said, that the devil shall be tormented forever and ever in the lake of fire and brimstone, where are the beast or the worshippers of idols, and the false prophet or all the friends and propagators of error. This is represented as taking place immediately before the final judgment, at the close of which transaction, whosoever is not found written in the book of life will be cast into the same place of torment. The *lake of fire* therefore denotes the punishment which is elsewhere denominated *hell-fire*, the *furnace of fire*, *outer darkness* and *everlasting fire*. And what other sense can here be attached to *aion*, translated forever, but endless duration? It does not mean the universe, it does not mean the things of this world, it does not mean the age anterior to the Messiah's reign; it must, therefore, mean that which is to come, or all future time, for this is its only remaining signification. The other passage, in which *aion* is used in reference to future punishment, is in the third chapter of St. Mark. "But he that shall blaspheme against the Holy Ghost, hath *never* forgiveness, but is in danger of eternal damnation." *Aion* here occurs in the phrase, " hath never forgiveness." The word, translated eternal in the last clause of the verse, is *aionios*. They are evidently used as synonymous, the sentiment being repeated for the sake of intensity. But he that shall blaspheme against the Holy Ghost, hath not forgiveness *forever*, but is deserving of *eternal damnation*. That an absolute eternity is meant, a parallel passage sufficiently demonstrates by asserting, that such blasphemers shall be forgiven neither in this world neither in the world to come. Nothing now remains. but to sum up the argument contained in the texts in favor of endless punishment. If the passages themselves are examined, they lead to the belief that aion is used in the endless sense, and if its original and common import is to be regarded, the same conclusion is established. Hence it appears, that lost men will never be restored to virtue and happiness.

2. *Aionios* is found in the New Testament in seventy-one passages. In sixty of these it is applied, either to God, to heaven, to the happiness of the righteous, or to the gospel or kingdom of Christ, in such a manner as must be admitted to imply an endless duration. In six of the remaining passages, only eleven in all, it is used with reference to future punishment. The other five I shall now transcribe, that each may judge for himself, whether an eternal duration is not signified. " Who hath saved us, and called us with a holy calling, not according to our works, but according to his own purpose and grace, which was given us in Christ Jesus *before the world began*," or from eternity. " In hope of eternal life, which God that cannot lie, promised *before the world began*," or from eternity. " Now to him that

2 Timothy, i. 9. Titus, i. 2.

is of power to establish you, according to my
gospel, and the preaching of Jesus Christ, according to the revelation of the mystery, which
was kept secret *since the world began*," or from
eternity. " For perhaps he therefore departed for a season, that thou shouldest receive
him *forever*." Here the apostle has reference
to the relation in which Philemon and Onesi-
mus stood to each other in consequence of
their common faith. a relation which shall
never be broken. "Of the doctrine of bap-
tisms, and of laying on of hands, and of resurrection of the dead, and of *eternal* judgment," a
judgment the consequences of which are eternal. It may then safely be asserted, that
aionios is never used in the New Testament
except for unlimited duration either past or
future. Unless some reason is assigned for
attaching to it a signification found no where
else, it is to be thus understood when applied
to future punishment. It is natural in this
place to express no small surprise, that it
should so often be asserted both orally and from
the press, that an absolute eternity is not denoted by aionios. It cannot be shown to have any

Romans, xvi. 25. Philemon, 15. Hebrews. vi. 2.
12 *

other sense in the whole New Testament. This is its universal meaning, unless it is to be restricted when employed in reference to the single subject of future punishment. And is it credible, that Christ and his apostles use it on all other topics in the endless sense, and in this alone to express a limited time? This they must believe, who contend for the restoration of the wicked. If, when applied to future punishment, it denotes a temporary duration, the evidence is to be found in the context where it occurs, or in the nature of the subject itself. But the subject certainly admits as possible the doctrine of endless punishment. To an examination of aionios in this particular application, it is now proposed to attend; which will show conclusively, that no reason exists for limiting its signification in these cases. On the contrary, new considerations will be suggested for understanding it in its original and common import. These texts occur in the eighteenth and twenty-fifth chapters of Matthew, in the third chapter of St. Mark, in the first chapter of the second epistle to the Thessalonians, and in the epistle of Jude. That in Mark was noticed while examining the passages in which *aion* is applied to future punishment. "But he that shall blaspheme against the Holy Ghost, hath never forgiveness, but is in danger of *eternal* damnation." In this case, there is not only no reason for supposing that it departs from its usual meaning, but much, on account of the corresponding assertion "hath never forgiveness," to conclude, that it is used in an endless sense. Its import is equally obvious in the following construction. "Wherefore, if thy hand or thy foot offend thee, cut them off, and cast them from thee; it is better for thee to enter into life halt or maimed, rather than having two hands or two feet to be cast into *everlasting* fire. And if thine eye offend thee, pluck it out, and cast it from thee; it is better for thee, to enter into life with one eye, rather than having two eyes, to be cast into *hell-fire*." The two remaining instances in which it occurs in St. Matthew, are still more decisive. "Then shall he say also unto them on the left hand, depart from me, ye cursed, into *everlasting fire*, prepared for the devil and his angels." Here aionios may certainly bear the endless sense. No intimation is given why it should be limited. "And these shall go away into *everlasting punishment*, but the righteous into *life eternal.*" It is twice used in this verse, once in reference to the happiness of heaven, and once in reference to the miseries of hell. The two states are directly contrasted. *These shall go away into punishment eternal, but the righteous into life eternal.* What can be the plea for rendering aionios in one case in the endless sense, and for restricting it in the other to finite duration? There can be none. The principles of interpretation, on the contrary, require the same signification in both parts of the antithesis. So obvious is this, that if it most commonly denotes a temporal duration, it demands the the endless sense in this place. It cannot express in the first clause any thing less than eternal punishment, if it expresses eternal happiness in the second. The passage in the epistle to the Thessalonians, is an equally explicit proof of endless punishment. " When the Lord Jesus shall be revealed from heaven, with his mighty angels, in flaming fire, taking vengeance on them that know not God, and obey not the gospel of our Lord Jesus Christ; who shall be punished with *everlasting* destruction from the presence of the Lord, and from the glory of his power."

Nothing requires us to limit the signification of aionios in this case, rather than in others where the happiness of the righteous is the subject of discourse. In the epistle of Jude occurs the last of these passages. " Even as Sodom and Gomorrah and the cities about them in like manner, giving themselves over to fornication, and going after strange flesh, are set forth for an example, suffering the vengeance of *eternal* fire." The writer speaks in the preceding verse of the confinement of the fallen angels in *everlasting* chains, and immediately adds :—" *even as* Sodom and Gomorrah **** are set forth for an example, suffering the vengeance of *eternal* fire." This shows that the fire, which is declared to be eternal, or according to the usual sense of aionios *endless*, is the fire of hell. As no reason can be given for understanding it differently, this sense must be admitted; whence the argument from the use of aionios appears complete and unanswerable. It can neither be said, that its common meaning, or the particular manner in which it is applied to future punishment allow, much less require it to be understood in a temporary sense. The conclusion is much more irresistible in this case, than when it is drawn from the signification of *aion*, where a contrary use may be pleaded. But it has been shown, that even in that case the argument is very satisfactory in favor of eternal punishment. Nor can the evidence be diminished, by referring to the prevailing notions of the Pharisees and Essenes on the subject. They believed in eternal punishment, but Christ did not surely teach it in compliance with their prejudices. Had they been in an error, instead of affording the sanction of his authority, he would have warned them against it. Nor is it satisfactory to say, that the language is parabolic and must not be too much pressed; that Christ only means that men shall be judged and rewarded according to their works. The language is *not pressed*, when it is literally interpreted, especially when the connexion defines the meaning. Whoever then is disposed to admit the declaration of God as certain evidence, will confess that the doctrine of eternal punishment is true.

IV. *That lost men will never be restored to the divine favor appears from many other explicit assertions.* In proof of this, I subjoin the following.

1. " That which beareth thorns and briers

is rejected, and is nigh unto cursing: whose *end* is to be burned." "For many walk, of whom I have told you often, and now tell you even weeping, that they are the enemies of the cross of Christ; whose *end* is destruction." "And no marvel; for Satan himself is transformed into an angel of light. Therefore it is no great thing, if his ministers also be transformed, as the ministers of righteousness; whose *end* shall be according to their works," which are surely evil. By such declarations the final condemnation of the wicked, is as clearly taught as it can be. Their *end* is to be burned, their *end* is destruction, their *end* is according to their works. How then can their *end* be salvation? To say that the *end* here spoken of, is not their last end is an assertion without proof.

2. "The preaching of the cross is to them that *perish*, foolishness; but unto us, who are saved, it is the power of God.' "And shall *utterly perish* in their own corruption." "For what is a man advantaged, if he gain the whole world and *lose himself*, or be *cast away*." "On whomsoever it shall fall, it will

Hebrews, vi. 8.   Phillippians iii. 18.   2 Corinthians, xi. 14, 15.
1 Corinthians, i. 18.   2 Peter, ii. 12.   Luke, ix. 25.

grind him to powder." "For wide is the gate
and broad is the way, that leadeth to *destruction."* " If our gospel be hid, it is hid to them
that are *lost."* Every reader of the bible
knows how inconsistent such language is with
the doctrine of restoration. To be cast away,
lost, destroyed, rejected, is in scripture always
put in opposition to salvation. But where is
the opposition, if those who perish are to be
saved?

3. " Wo unto you that are rich; for ye have
received your *consolation."* " Son, remember,
that thou *in thy life time* received *thy good
things."* " For I say unto you, that none of
those men which were bidden shall taste of my
supper." " He that believeth not the Son,
shall *not see life,* but the wrath of God *abideth*
on him." " He that is unjust, let him be unjust still; and he which is filthy, let him be
filthy still." How can it be said that the rich
receive their consolation in this life, if they
are to receive abundantly more in the next?
How can it be said of Dives, that he received
his good things on earth, if he is destined to a
far richer inheritance in heaven? How can

Matthew, xxi. 44.　vii. 13.　2. Corinthians, iv. 3.　Luke, vi.
24. xvi. 25.　xiv. 24.　John iii. 36.　Rev. xxii. 11.

it be said, that those who refuse the invitations of God to the supper of his Son, that is, to celestial enjoyments, shall never taste of that supper, if they are notwithstanding to be saved? How can it be said that he, who believeth not the Son, shall not see life (shall not enjoy the happiness of heaven) if he is ultimately to escape from punishment? How can it be said, that the wrath of God shall abide upon him, if it is ever to be withdrawn? How can the filthy be filthy still, if they are to become holy and happy? All such declarations it must be admitted, teach eternal punishment.

This protracted, but I hope profitable investigation, is now closed. Other things relating to the general subject, are yet to be considered, but the unreasonableness of expecting the restoration of lost men to virtue and happiness, is now made sufficiently apparent. Many other passages might be named, which convey the same unequivocal testimony in favor of this conclusion, but unless you are willing to believe the inspired declarations already exhibited, you will not assent to any evidence whatever. " And he said unto him; —If they hear not Moses and the prophets, neither will they be persuaded, though one rose from the dead." Indeed, what more can you desire? How various, express and abundant are the proofs before you! There is scarcely any other subject in the bible, so much noticed, or on which there are such explicit revelations. Apply the common rules for interpreting language to the passages which speak of the duration of future punishment, and the conclusion that it is everlasting, cannot be evaded. And why do you, my hearer, refuse your assent to the doctrine? You can offer no satisfactory reason. The bible makes no contradictory statements on this subject. The evidence already advanced, is a fair example of the manner in which the doctrine is treated throughout the word of God. Why then do you not believe? I know the reason. *It is an awful truth.* You shrink from the dreadful necessity of admitting it, as you would from the sentence of death. You consequently flatter yourself that it is inconsistent with the character of God. But did you gain such an idea of Him, from his works and providence? How could you? He allows sin and misery to exist in this world. Judging of what he may do, from what he has done, it is surely not impossible that suffering will never cease under his government. Where then have you learned that He is too good to punish the wicked? God is indeed infinitely good—He himself asserts it. But if you believe this, why will you not believe when he asserts that the wicked shall be punished forever? Is one of his declarations more worthy of credit than another? But he has never informed you that he is too good to inflict eternal punishment. You have not learned in the bible that this is his character. Where then did you obtain this extraordinary acquaintance with your Maker? You obtained it no where. There is no such God as your imagination has conceived. The fact that you would save all men of every description of character, is no evidence that He will. You would restore your dying neighbor to health, relieve his wife from the agony of separation and his children from orphanage and want; but the most merciful God decides differently, and allows disease, poverty and death to fill the world with tears and suffering. No benevolent man would be the author of so much misery. The unlimited knowledge of God enables him to perceive equity, wisdom and goodness in events which no human being would imagine, without a revelation, to be either kind or just. Such is the nature of eternal punishment. It is an order of God's government inseparable from the most important interests of his kingdom, and which he will maintain, however much the sympathies of our frail and erring nature may revolt at its execution. Why then do you not credit the frequent and explicit testimony of his word on this momentous subject? What do you gain by your ceaseless efforts to evade the truth, by your unprofitable zeal in disseminating error? What advantage have you even now, in the things whereof you will one day be ashamed? I put the question to excite reflection. The condemnation to which sin exposes us, may be avoided by repentance. God has appointed a day in which he will judge the secrets of men, by that man whom he hath ordained; on which account, he commands all men to repent, as an adequate and indispensable security against the sentence of indignation and wrath. But he, who denies the justice and possibility of everlasting punishment, makes himself ignorant of the nature and tendency of sin, ignorant of his own character and of his God; for he beholds not the moral image of man reflected from the lake of despair, and turns not with contrition and gratitude to the cross of Christ. The evidence which he smothers, the light which he extinguishes, is essential to his pardon and eternal peace. " Consider this, ye that forget God, lest I tear you in pieces, and there be none to deliver."

LECTURE VII.

THE NATURE OF FUTURE PUNISHMENT.

—●●●●—

MATTHEW xxv. 30.

And cast ye the unprofitable servant into outer darkness : there shall be weeping and gnashing of teeth.

ERRONEOUS views and destructive prejudices have extensively prevailed in consequence of misunderstanding the language of the bible in reference to future punishment. Are the wicked to be literally destroyed ? is their existence to terminate with this life ? are their sufferings merely mental ? are they to be punished in flames of fire ? These questions which have been agitated with much interest, and which have received various solutions, it is the design of this discourse to answer.

I. *Future punishment does not consist in annihilation.* Such a conclusion, the literal import of destruction, of perishing, of perdition, justifies. " Who shall be punished with everlasting destruction." " And shall utterly perish in their own corruption." But the expressions are figurative. They do not denote an abolition or annihilation of the soul, but moral ruin or the destruction of character and happiness. The same usage prevails in all languages. They are often said to be destroyed, who are only ruined in reputation, property and influence. That the literal sense of such terms is not applicable to future punishment, appears from the distinctions which are made in its degrees of severity, and from numerous expressions which represent lost men to be in a state of conscious existence. It is also found from an examination of the phraseology in question, that it is obviously used by the sacred writers in a metaphorical sense. " Whose judgment now a long time lingereth not, and their damnation (destruction) slumbereth not." The apostle refers to a punishment to be inflicted at the judgment day, when God will display his indignation by a marked distinction in its degrees of severity. " But *chiefly* them that walk after the flesh, in the lust of concupiscence and despise government.''

Destruction occurs in the same sense in the ninth chapter of Romans;—" What, if God willing to show his wrath and make his power known, endured with much long-suffering the vessels of wrath fitted to destruction." So far from rendering his wrath and power conspicuous by suspending an act of annihilation, God would forcibly illustrate both by an immediate execution But if destruction signifies the infliction of pain, the sense is clear and impressive. Through the forbearance of God, the wicked have an opportunity of filling up, in their voluntary and inexcusable rebellion, the measure of their iniquities and of fitting themselves to be more striking examples of his displeasure against sin and of his power to punish it.

II. *No phraseology of the bible exactly defines the nature of future punishment.* We are not expressly informed in what it consists. Many persons however consider the language descriptive of the misery of lost men as philosophical definitions. We find in the history of fanaticism, women plucking out their eyes and cutting off their hands in supposed obedience to our Savior's command;—· If thine eye offend thee, pluck it out, if thine hand or foot

offend thee, cut it off.' The mind without
training, is prone to stop at the literal import
of words, and never to take their secondary or
figurative sense. We speak of the future
world in the language of the bible and in the
sense of the sacred writers, not meaning that
hell is literally a furnace of fire, but only that
its sufferings are intense. The style of the
language however makes the impression very
extensive, that the pains of hell are exactly
such as fire produces. Although our meaning is frequently explained, we cannot always
guard against misapprehension, especially in
the case of transient hearers. Hence the
minds of ignorant men are sometimes embit-
tered against the truth, by the suspicion that
its teachers believe in the existence of a furnace of material fire and brimstone. But
orthodox divines decide unanimously, that no
literal and precise account of the condition of
lost men is given in the bible. Their reasons
shall now be stated.

'1. *Analogy makes it probable, that the descriptions of future punishment are figurative.* Heaven
is a place ineffably glorious and happy. We
are taught its splendor, under the similitude of
a city constructed of the richest materials

and in the most magnificent style; and its amenity, salubriousness and abundance, under the figure of a garden irrigated by perennial waters, warmed by a genial sun and yielding all kinds of delicious fruits. None interpret the language literally; no one imagines that any thing definite is known of spiritual existence or of the modes of enjoyment in that world. It is a place of great glory, of spotless purity and of unsullied serenity and bliss: but it is not revealed how its inhabitants receive and communicate ideas, how they pursue pleasing employments, how God and angels appear in immediate vision. If you thus judge of the heavenly world, why not apply the same rule of interpretation to descriptions of the place of punishment? why not regard them as intended to convey only a vivid picture of misery?

2. *Almost all that is said of future existence must be in the language of approximation.* The invisible world cannot be described except by comparison with things seen. If it is not in its modes of feeling and acting like what we here experience, a philosophical knowledge of it is unattainable.

3. *The nature of spiritual existence, so far as*

it is understood, is inconsistent with the literal import of the descriptions of future punishment. Of the organization of the soul and of its spiritual body we know nothing, except that it depends not on animal attractions or is not subject to the laws of flesh and blood. This negative knowledge affords assurance, that the same modes of pleasure and of pain will not prevail in both states of existence. Bodies differently constructed and under the control of different laws, are not susceptible of the same sensations from the same causes. Fire occasions pain by its chemical action in varying or disorganizing the structure of the animal system, which process cannot be predicated of a spiritual body which is immortal and consequently indestructible.

4. *The same forms of description are employed in reference to the dead before the resurrection while in an unembodied state.* " The rich man also died, and was buried, and in hell he lifted up his eyes being in torments, and seeth Abraham afar off, and Lazarus in his bosom. And he cried and said, Father Abraham, have mercy on me, and send Lazarus that he may dip the tip of his finger in water and cool my tongue, for I am tormented in this flame."

Here almost every particular is enumerated, which enters into the descriptions of future punishment. The rich man in hell is represented as possessing the members, passions and sensibilities of a material body and as subjected to the action of a material element. But he was not in a body, either animal or spiritual, whence the representation is evidently figurative.

5. *If the language of the sacred writers in reference to the sufferings of hell are literal, they are contradictory.* This remarkable passage in St. Mark is inconsistent with itself;—" And if thy hand offend thee, cut it off: it is better for thee to enter into life maimed, than having two hands to go into hell, into the fire that never shall be quenched: where their worm dieth not, and the fire is not quenched." The points of discrepancy are the *worm that never dies* and *the fire that is never quenched*, circumstances which cannot co-exist. The description in the text is equally decisive. "Cast ye the unprofitable servant into outer darkness ;—there shall be weeping and gnashing of teeth." This gives a horrible picture of the lonely and dismal condition of lost men. But if it is *literally* true, if they are *actually*

in *darkness*, how can other phraseology applied to future punishment be explained? A world lighted up by everlasting flames cannot be a place of darkness. It is thus that we infer that descriptions of heaven are figurative. In one place God is represented as dwelling in light unapproachable and full of glory, and in another as making darkness his pavilion. These accounts are in the letter contradictory, but in their real import harmonious. They mean only that He cannot be seen and fully comprehended. Thus the various and apparently irreconcilable accounts which we have of hell, appear perfectly correct. They are only intended to teach that the place is extremely miserable and appalling.

III. *Although a literal account of the nature of future punishment is not given, we partly know in what it consists from the properties of the human mind.*

1. *Lost men will be harassed with discontent.* The love of happiness is inseparable from their nature. While beholding the blessedness of heaven and feeling a total deprivation of the means of enjoyment, they will be tormented with ungratified desire. Dissatisfac-

tion with existing circumstances and fruitless wishes for a change which they cannot enjoy, will keep them in perpetual irritation. There can be nothing tranquil and serene where there is nothing to allay vexation, and where every thing to excite it abounds. To be where all bad principles, where all unholy feelings burn and rage without restraint, where they are all inflamed by a sense of want, and of ignominy, and by a view of the blessedness of heaven, in which spirits originally of a nature like its own are exulting in perfect holiness, will deprive the soul of tranquillity and contentment, and call every angry passion into exercise. Envy, hatred and revenge, which were once in their infancy and only excited at intervals, will gather strength from free indulgence, and exasperation from the poverty and despair of its circumstances. Its desires can never be satisfied, its malice never accomplished, its revenge never satiated. Such turbulence and dissatisfaction, the reality of which is fairly inferred from the nature of the mind, will undoubtedly contribute to the miseries of lost men.

2. *Recollection will awaken the anguish of unmingled self-reproach, of the most bitter regret*

and of biting remorse. The wretched soul will remember its abused sabbaths, its stifled convictions, its broken vows, its vicious practices, its half formed resolutions of amendment. its neglected bible and slighted opportunities, with shame and dismay. Every moment, which recalls such acts of folly and guilt, will be replete with anguish. Then light will fall on each step of probationary existence. Sins before unsuspected or forgotten, will flash on the mind. The justice of God will be relieved from suspicion. The soul will not doubt that mortal life was short, its joys mean and its concerns trifling, in comparison with the interests of an endless existence. It will stand in amazement at the folly which for the honor, ease and pleasures of earth provoked the wrath of God and forfeited heaven. It will not recall one event or act of life on which to reflect with satisfaction. The past will only flash on the mind to keep open an eternal wound. Endeavor to picture in imagination a being cut off from friendship, from peace and pleasant occupation and confined in dismal abodes, with no employment but meditation on past existence, and that existence replete with events, at the remembrance of which he is overwhelmed with shame, remorse and anguish. Imagine yourself in his stead, a lonely, blasted, and haggard outcast, unpitied and unprotected, with no subject of reflection but the crimes and follies which have thus reduced you! What could create more exquisite suffering than the recollection of those deeds of madness which drew you from probationary ground into utter ruin? How painful to retrace the steps by which you approached the gulf of despair! how painful to remember duties unperformed, opportunities unregarded, proffered pardon often despised and salutary fears always quelled!

3. *Despair of a better state will deprive the sufferings of hell of mitigation, and form one of its most appalling circumstances.* To feel that their condition is unalterable, their portion unalienable, that the night of darkness on which they entered at death has no morning, that the fire into which they are banished is unquenchable, that the worms which prey on their spirits never die, is the dreadful doom of lost men. Could ages bring them relief, though wrapt in mantles of woe and lying on beds of sorrow, they might wait patiently.

But no such expectation sustains them in the midst of their miseries. They are no longer deceived by error, no longer consoled by hope. They are persuaded of the awful truth;—as the tree falls, so it lies. It is impossible for us to realize this state of mind. To be involved in wretchedness which we know will never cease, to see the frown of God, to look back and forward without fixing on one object to relieve, and in full expectancy of worse evils, is hell. In this life we know nothing of it. Here in the saddest conjunctures, when every friend forsakes us and every prospect lowers, we look to all changing time, and hope for succor. But in hell the storm never clears away, the sunshine of prosperity never opens upon the soul, the expectation of a brighter day is over. It is not wonderful that in this state of feeling, the agitated and despairing spirit should exclaim ;—

> " Which way shall I fly ?
> Infinite wrath and infinite despair !
> Which way I fly is hell, myself an hell ;—
> And in the lowest deep, a lower deep,
> Still threatening to devour me, opens wide,
> To which the hell I suffer seems a heaven."

The evil that it now experiences it could

14 *

brace itself to bear, but the abysses into which it must yet descend, the long tracks of misery it must yet travel, the horrid conviction it must yet so often feel that the work of destruction is only now begun, makes it feel that it is indeed in Hell.

4. But there are other modes of wretchedness which we may justly ascribe to the inhabitants of that world. The stings of conscience, the gnawings of remorse, the agitations of passion, the bitterness of recollection and sickening despair, are not the only messengers of wrath to execute the penalties of God's violated law. *Satan and his angels and lost men themselves are the executors of his will.* You might as well look for harmony in the abodes of maddened insanity, as among spirits infuriated by crime and anguish. If love is the harmony of heaven, enmity must make discord in hell. The wicked are selfish ; no law of benevolence binds them in communities for mutual benefit, no principles of justice protect them from mutual aggression. What will not passion, unbridled and exasperated do among the miserable victims of despair ? When will the hatred of such beings cease, when will their conflicts end, when will order be

restored where confusion reigns, when will the tumult and collision of mutual hostility terminate? Who could wish a habitation, who could endure even a visit in that world of darkness, of despair, and of malevolence?

5. But the most dreadful circumstance in the sentence of damnation has not yet been named. *I mean the wrath of the Lamb.* Conscious of having incurred the displeasure of a just and and merciful being, the wicked must look at themselves with shame, at each other with scorn, and to heaven with consternation. To behold the Lamb of God whom they have treated with indignity, quitting the mercy seat and assuming the throne of justice, to behold a frown where once pity sat, to hear sounds of vengeance from lips which once uttered love, and to know that by their own obduracy they have rendered this change necessary and just, closes in a most dreadful climax all that we can positively assert of their miseries. From the nature of their minds and from the characters which they sustain, it is probable that fretful, angry and vindictive passions, painful recollections, fiend-like animosities, and heart-chilling anticipations, conscious guilt, remorse and fell despair, will form part of the

degradation and anguish of destruction. By what other means the soul will be made to feel the evil of sin, and to deplore its own perversity, cannot here be ascertained. Nor could any important object be secured by a more precise and definite acquaintance with the modes of future punishment. The design of revelation is to protect the law of God from violation. We are therefore informed that its sanctions are severe. To impress this on the mind, the most terrific descriptions of the world of punishment that language affords are employed. But still they may prove to be only approximations to the truth. By means as yet unknown the anguish of the soul may be increased beyond present conception, and to a degree never expressed in words. Its distress will certainly equal whatever is implied in lying down in devouring fire and in everlasting burnings.

LECTURE VIII.

THE JUSTICE OF FUTURE PUNISHMENT.

ROMANS iii. 5.

Is God unrighteous who taketh vengeance ?

THE conclusions to which we have arrived in the preceding lectures, are asserted to be inconsistent with the justice of God. The grounds on which this opinion rests, shall be examined after some direct evidence is offered in opposition to the objection itself.

1. *Eternal punishment cannot be pronounced unjust, because it is impossible to show that the wicked can be made to submit to the government of God.* None will deny, that so long as they persevere in opposition to their Maker, their condemnation is perfectly equitable. It is only on the supposition that they will imbibe a better spirit, that their sentence can be considered too severe. It therefore devolves

upon the objector to prove that the sufferings
of hell are disciplinary, and better adapted
than any means here enjoyed to subdue the
heart to the love and fear of God, and that
this will actually be the effect. This he cannot do. So far as we understand the tendency
of punishment, it affords no reason to expect
repentance after death. The soul is never
terrified into obedience. It is indeed often
induced to seek security by the apprehension
of danger. But though there may be a com-
mencement of serious solicitude and inquiry
in consequence of the threatenings of God
against transgressors, there never was and
there never can be a mind softened and sub-
dued by fear. If a person finds himself subjected to excruciating sufferings, and involved
in the fear of greater in consequence of his
sins, his heart rises against God, he feels
indignant that he should be so severely,
and as he thinks, so injuriously treated.
However powerful may be his convictions of guilt, and however real the danger may appear. it is not till he has seen
the Lamb of God, that the stubbornness
of his mind begins to yield. He must have a
view of the love and compassion of Christ,

before he will humbly acknowledge his sinfulness and accept of mercy. We know from these facts, that persons dying in their sins will have no more disposition to repent afterwards than they had in this life, nor probably as much. They may then feel what they here anticipated. with as little beneficial effect, and with more virulent opposition. Their sinful preferences will probably continue with unabated strength through every step of existence. It would be of no avail to proffer them pardon under the condition of reconciliation to God with which they will never comply. But can that punishment be otherwise than just, which is rendered necessary by the obstinate perversity of the sufferer?

2. *Eternal punishment cannot be pronounced unjust, since it is impossible to show, that the interests which sin tends to destroy and which such a penalty alone can protect. are not of corresponding importance.* The punishment which God inflicts is always exactly proportioned to the guilt of the sufferer. which is ascertained by the damage done to the universe by transgression. We have no measure of the evil of sin, excepting so far as we are acquainted with the interest which it threatens to annihilate.

But it is impossible to decide, that these interests are not of a nature to justify eternal punishment, and that their protection does not demand it. The welfare of the universe is to be principally considered, in all the measures of the divine sovereignty. Minds little accustomed to think, do not always perceive how essential it is to intelligent creatures at large, that transgressions be noticed by exemplary punishments. Moral beings are so under the control of what they consider desirable or otherwise, that unless the apparent value of unlawful pleasures is overbalanced by penalties against them, they will transgress. How unsuccessfully would God endeavor to secure their obedience were they left without one personal inducement to keep his commandments! Had the sanctions of the law never been executed, the rebellion which is now limited might have become co extensive with the rational creation. We may confidently assert, that no reformation would take place, that where apostacy once began it would be perpetual. Not an individual could be redeemed by Jesus Christ, for no one would acknowledge his guilt, no one would feel his necessities, no one would sue for mercy.

Since disobedience to the law of God is destructive of such incalculable interests, producing of itself everlasting degradation and misery, and threatening to carry ruin throughout the universe, it seems indubitable that eternal punishment is only an equitable vindication of the law. The objector will certainly find it a fruitless attempt to show, that sin does not tend to destroy a greater degree of happiness, than is sacrificed in the eternal misery of incorrigible offenders. If by breaking the laws of God, we endanger interests which are more valuable than our individual happiness, and which eternal punishment can alone secure, sin merits such a penalty. This supposition cannot be shown unfounded, and consequently it is impossible to pronounce the doctrine which we have established, untrue.

3. *Eternal punishment is just, because God will execute it.* It is on this ground that the apostle replies to the interrogation;—"Is God unrighteous, who taketh vengeance? God forbid, for how then shall God judge the world." He assumes it for granted, that the wicked will be punished. The obvious inference is

15

that they deserve it. Men are apt to reason differently. Because God is just, they infer that he will not punish. The apostle, on the contrary, concludes from the righteousness of God, that the punishment which he has threatened, and which he will inflict is just; and this undoubtedly is the only correct mode of reasoning. We cannot tell what God may justly do in relation to human wickedness, until he reveals his own determination. The excellence of his character is so undoubted that whatever he informs us will be his conduct, we must conclude is fit and equitable. ·

The objection to the doctrine of future punishment, founded on the justice of God, is therefore untenable. It cannot be proved, that lost men will repent or that they are undeserving of eternal punishment, while the declaration of God, that they shall suffer thus, is a positive proof of its equity.

It only remains to examine the grounds on which the objection rests, and from which it receives its plausibility.

I. *It is urged as an act of injustice to punish those who never consented to be put on trial.* But is this **true?** Is consent necessary to the ex-

istence of obligation? The child is bound
to obey its parents, though it never assumed
the obligation by voluntary agreement. Men
are often laid under obligations of gratitude
by benefits which were conferred without
their request, and without the possibility of
avoiding them. Even those who assert
as an objection to eternal punishment, that
they were put on trial without their consent, admit that they owe certain duties
to God, as love, adoration and gratitude.
But whence does this obligation arise
and on what is it founded? Did God con-
sult us, whether we would be objects of
his peculiar regard and munificence? Did
we consent to be born under happy auspices,
in a christian country, in a land of freedom
and in an age of peculiar light? or were any
of our ordinary blessings proffered and accept-
ed, before we were under obligation? Certainly not. On their own principles then, the
argument of these men fails. If we are without our consent under obligations to serve
God, we are responsible, and obnoxious to
punishment for disobedience.

II. *The manner in which sin found entrance
into the world through Adam, is represented to be*

inconsistent with justice in the punishment of his posterity. It is true that we stand related to our first parents in a sense which effects our dearest interests. " By the offence of one, judgment came upon all men to condemnation." But God has not treated us unjustly nor unkindly. On the contrary, by passing the sentence of condemnation which Adam incurred upon the whole race, He opened the way for introducing the plan of redemption, and for placing mankind in a better condition, than that which was forfeited by the first offence. This position appears with high probability to be true, from the following considerations.

1. *The posterity of Adam are in a condition preferable to that which they lost by his offence.* At first his circumstances appeared fair and promising. He was the friend of God. The garden was fitted up for his residence with every thing to regale his senses, enlist his mind and delight his heart. He had nothing to fear, except the slight temptation which was to test his obedience. But amid all this display of his Maker's power and goodness, he fell. At the very moment when he was in the full enjoyment of his dominions, and per-

haps in sweet converse with heaven, the tempter was laying a plot to beguile him. The trial proved fatal. The experiment however was a fair one, and shows that it is infinitely dangerous for a being like man, to be placed under a system of mere law. Now though we are in danger, we are not in despair. But had we been left under law, and exposed in the same way that Adam was, being in no more eligible circumstances and having no more power of resistance, we should have sinned without the least prospect of escaping the execution of justice. We should have been cast off like the fallen angels. No invitation of mercy would have reached our ears, no blood would have washed away our guilt. The condition, therefore, which Adam occupied and which we lost by him, was one of greater danger than that in which by the sacrifice of Jesus Christ we are now placed.

2. *A state of trial under a system of mere law, such as the angels and our first parents experienced, is never so desirable as one under a system of grace.*

In the former case, a single offence is fatal, in the latter, the vilest offender can escape.

And even supposing it possible, that he who is under law *may* never sin, while he who is under grace has already done it, the condition of the latter is most to be desired. He has only to comply with the terms of the covenant of grace, which terms must from the nature of the case be possible, and the deadly consequences of his sin are at once averted. But when one under mere law offends, he is left without hope. Nothing can save him. If, therefore, it is possible, especially if it is probable, that he will sin, his condition becomes inconceivably more dangerous than that of the actual sinner, to whom pardon is proffered. Adam, created in the moral image of God, and for sometime obedient, at last fell, and had it not been for grace would have perished; but Enoch, made in a fallen state and guilty of actual sin, walked by faith and was not, for God took him. I know, indeed, there is great danger of perishing, even where grace abounds. I only contend that the prospect and entire opportunity of being saved, is to be preferred to a state of probation, where disobedience is possible and always fatal. This opportunity every man under the christian dispensation enjoys, but when put on trial with this condition—do and live, disobey and die—he might by some sudden attack of the enemy be cast from the happy kingdom of God into remediless ruin.

3. *Had we sustained no moral relation to Adam and received from him no bad influence whatever, we should have been exposed to sin and probably should have fallen.*

Perhaps Adam only fixed the seal of certainty to what was otherwise highly probable. If this can be proved, it will be evident that Christ has advanced us to a condition vastly more to be desired than that which we lost by the common parents of mankind. By asserting it, I know I take a bold position. Some have even supposed, that had Adam remained obedient when tempted to eat the forbidden fruit, both he and his posterity would have been confirmed in a state of holiness. But this is a gratuitous supposition. It is not taught in the word of God, it is totally without support. True, the moral powers gain strength by exercise, and as far as Adam himself was concerned, an act of obedience would afford evidence of his continuing loyal. But no such influence could reach his posterity. Besides, the whole analogy of providence is against this hypothesis. Adam was put on trial for himself, Eve for herself, angels for themselves, and we for ourselves. We know of no moral agent, except God himself, who has not been tried. Even Christ was in all points tempted like as we are. Indeed, I know not, that trial is separable from the moral agency of creatures. Place a being in circumstances where he never has the slightest incitement to evil, where either he has not the ability or the opportunity to choose what is wrong, and his conduct will be destitute both of praise and blame, neither an object of censure nor complacency. Hence we must have been put on probation and by our own choice have determined for ourselves the question of happiness or misery. Indeed whatever evidence this subject admits, is entirely in the face of the idea of confirmation in holiness extended to us in consideration of another's obedience. But that we should have probably fallen, though unaffected by Adam, may be gathered from several independent facts.

God has given evidence, that he considers the fall of Adam as a fair trial of what might be expected from his descendants should each act for himself.

As soon as Adam sinned, both he and his posterity felt the rigour of the law. The gates of paradise were closed against the whole race. The procedure is no more directed at him than at his unborn and unoffending offspring. When he fell as the fact declares, all fell. But how does this consist with the justice of God? Plainly, because the fate of Adam was indicative of what would happen to all men, when in no more favorable circumstances and endowed with no superior powers. But God had done all for him which he wisely could do, and of course as much as he could do for other men. "What could have been done more to my vineyard, that I have not done in it?" The result of this trial, however, was bad. Instead, therefore, of subjecting us to the same fatal ordeal, God passes the sentence of death upon *us* as well as upon him. But the justice of this procedure rests here, that Adam's trial is a fair experiment for us; that he did as we should have done, and therefore completely decided, what that would be. So God considered it. His treatment of the affair corresponds with such a supposition. To this it may be added, *that we should have been more powerfully tempted*

with less power of resistance than Adam had.
The truth of this may be disputed. I would
by no means affirm it as demonstrable. Were
it so, no doubt could remain, that all men
would have sinned even in paradise, and unaffected by their progenitors. The philosophy
of the mind makes it certain. But the argument which may be stated, is plausible, if not
entirely conclusive. The temptation of Adam
was a weak one. He took the forbidden
fruit to gratify an idle curiosity, not to satisfy
his necessities. He was in the midst of abundance. It is, too, so far as we know, the only
form of temptation with which he was ever
assailed. Compare his case in this respect with what, without theorizing, we may
suppose to be true of his posterity. They
were soon to be subjected to the trials which
result from a dense population whose interests
might clash, to circumstances where every
passion of animal nature and every power of
the soul might be attacked as inlets of vice.
It would be hard to conceive of a case, in
which they would be less forcibly tempted
than Adam was. These appeals, too, would
be almost as various as the objects and events
which caught their attention. If the first in-

citement to sin did not succeed, the second or the thousandth might; if an appeal to that passion failed, an appeal to this might drown the soul in perdition. In regard to our power of resistance compared with Adam's, it is absolutely demonstrable that it would have been less. He was created a man, capable of governing the lower creation, of fulfilling the duties of domestic life, of knowing God and engaging in his service. All this he actually did. His habits of obedience, his acquaintance with the pleasures of devotion, all that he had felt and done, volunteered to sustain him in his integrity. We on the other hand are created infants, without knowledge and without the advantage of fixed principles of virtue and of cultivated piety. Our minds are as fragile as our bodies. We have for a long time, little discrimination, little reflection, little caution. We are exposed to do wrong, long before we are capable of realizing anything like the extent of the consequences. All this is true, even had Adam remained obedient. The conclusion is obvious. We should have been eminently exposed to fall although uninfluenced by him. It will be difficult for any one to show, that all of us would not ultimately have perished without relief, had it pleased God to leave us unrelated to Adam and to Christ, uninjured by one and un-aided by the other. The argument is this. As God by his procedure with us has shown, that he considers Adam's conduct as a fair criterion of what ours would have been, and as the philosophy of the mind leads to the same conclusion, a great portion of mankind, if not all, would have sinned. All would have been exposed, and those who once fell lost forever. It follows, that the evil done us by Adam is trivial in comparison with the bless-ings which Christ has purchased with his precious blood. God has treated us kindly. He allowed Adam's fall to stand as ours, that he might avert the miseries which he foresaw we should otherwise bring upon ourselves, that he might introduce a system of grace and proffer pardon to all mankind. It was his design to offer mercy to all, to make salvation a thing optional with those who he saw would otherwise be irretrievably ruined.

4. *There are strong reasons for believing, that redeemed men will be much happier than they would have been, had they never sinned.* That they will have emotions, which grow directly

out of their relation to Christ and which are of the most delightful kind, no one can doubt. They will also have views of the character of God, peculiarly clear and peculiarly pleasing.

On the strength of the preceding considerations, may it not be confidently asked;—how can an objection to the doctrine of eternal punishment be drawn from the manner in which sin has been entailed, through the apostacy of the first man, upon his descendants? So far from being injured by such an arrangement, it becomes the means of our greatest benefit, so far from perishing on this account, it lays a foundation for the salvation of myriads of otherwise degraded and miserable sinners; so far from its being unjust to punish the guilty under such a system, it will aggravate the condemnation of all who do not reform.

III. *Eternal punishment is represented to be unjust, because God knew what characters men would sustain before he created them.* This objection proceeds on the false supposition, that the foreknowledge of God is inconsistent with human accountability. Were it so, it would be impossible for him to create a moral agent or to require the homage of any creature. But the persons, who offer this objection, admit the existence of obligation and of responsibility on the part of man, and the consequent sinfulness of the disobedient. They admit that transgression deserves punishment But how does this admission harmonize with the reason which they assign for not believing in endless punishment? If notwithstanding the foreknowledge of God, men expose themselves by sin to the vengeance of heaven, how does it render the eternal duration of punishment incredible? It certainly does not, unless it can be shown that the foresight of such tremendous consequences, would have suspended the act of creation. But who knows, that the system of things which God has preferred to every other, does not contain these consequences as necessary constituents, while at the same time every other possible plan is attended by worse results? If such is the fact, a foreknowledge of evils as great as are experienced can be no reason for refusing existence to the sufferers; for in that case God could not bring into being that system of things which supplies the greatest sum of happiness and which produces the least comparative evil. This objection, therefore, like the preceding, is unsustained and groundless.

IV. *It is urged against the justice of eternal punishment, that even the most wicked men perform some actions which God has promised to remunerate.* This objection results from ignorance of the extent and spirituality of the divine law. The love of God is the ruling motive in all actions, which are approved and rewarded. They are consequently peculiar to men of piety. "So then, they that are in the flesh cannot please God." "Without faith it is impossible to please him." "The carnal mind is enmity against God ; for it is not subject to the law of God, neither indeed can be." Christ frequently declares, that whosoever confers the least favor on his disciples, because they are such, shall in no wise lose his reward ; implying. that the actions which he approves, spring from religious motives, and are expressions of a pious heart. Accordingly in an account of the last judgment, he denies. that those on his left hand had ever performed any acceptable service, because their deeds of charity were not dictated by affection to him. "Inasmuch as ye did it not to one of the least of *these* (my brethren,) ye did it not to me." The reason is, that actions, which flow from the instincts of our nature, from the laws and customs of society, and other causes distinct from an intention of serving God, are destitute of an essential property of true obedience. The commands of God may be obeyed in their letter but not in their spirit, without a wish or expectation of gaining his favor, and without affording a single expression of attachment to him; as a man may accidentally do the will of another for whom he has no regard, and of whom he has even no knowledge. But there is no obedience in such acts—there is no design of pleasing God, and no satisfaction in the prospect of serving him; in consequence of which, the most amiable actions are destitute of that " holiness, without which no man shall see the Lord." Unbelievers do nothing which entitles them to the promises, or which is not justly disregarded in the decisions of the last tribunal, since they never act with a design and expectation of finding happiness in the service of their Maker.

V. *It is urged against the justice of eternal punishment, that it makes a greater difference in the allotments of men than their slight varieties of*

character justify.   But it should be remembered, that none are saved because they merit
the distinction, that none are acquitt´d except
through faith in Jesus Christ and in virtue of
his intercessions.   All men deserve eternal
punishment.   Those who renounce their sins,
submit to the government of God and accept
salvation, are advanced to unmerited honor
and blessedness, while all others by rejecting
these good tidings, exclude themselves from
heaven.   The mercy of God in saving the
penitent, does not make the punishment of
the impenitent unjust, but renders its equity
more conspicuous by showing that salvation
was proffered to all mankind.

From the justice, thus made apparent in
the eternal condemnation of the finally impenitent, I have one inference to make.
*That hope of heaven, which is not sustained
by a fair comparison between the heart and life,
and the conditions of salvation, is altogether fallacious.*   Were man blameless, he might claim
exemption from punishment, but having once
sinned, it is impossible for him to escape except by complying with the terms of the gospel.   Every well founded hope, therefore, depends, not on the justice and goodness of God

abstractly considered, but on discovering an agreement between the heart and the requirements of the bible. Unless an expectation of heaven is thus sustained, the benevolence and justice of God, are attributes full of terror. They make punishment the inevitable result of an unholy and impenitent life; they extinguish all hope, and fill the world of despair with weeping and gnashing of teeth. No madness on earth surpasses that of the unbeliever, who flatters himself with anticipations of heaven. God is just and good, therefore he will by no means clear the guilty. His attributes are pledged to maintain his law, and to protect his obedient subjects by the exemplary punishment of transgressors. There is nothing in his character which can afford them the least prospect of happiness, unless they become reconciled to him. Be not deceived. To live in hope of salvation without repentance and faith, is an act of desperation. Abandon your fallacious expectations before they abandon you, abandon them before the time elapses in which you may obtain that hope which is an anchor to the soul, and before you awake to the horrors of irretrievable disappointment. Then even the divine goodness will be more bitter than

death. The goodness of God! were it not
for that blest attribute, hell might almost put
on colors, and deck itself in habiliments of
festivity. It is that which fastens on the victim of his own crimes, and eats like the never
dying worm, and keeps in sensitive action, in
keen torture, every fibre of feeling. It
flashes on the mind the intense light of conviction, and wakes the peal of that heavy artillery
of vengeance, which drives the spirits of
lost men from the presence of a holy God. It
stands to sanction and enforce the stern decisions of justice. Then too, corruption of
character, become complete, will lay a foundation for unmittigated and endless anguish.
Every lost soul is like the confirmed and irre-
claimable victim of intemperance; the lamp of
reason extinguished, the sensibilities of the
heart chilled in eternal death, the will bent to
a perverse and unconquerable purpose, the
taste most impure, the passions most turbulent
and vile, the appetites most base and insatia-
ble, and all the issues of the soul abominable
and foul: there is no spring of reformation
that can be touched, no water of purification
that can suffice, no restorative which can al-
leviate. Behold how the disease has insinuat-
ed itself into the fountains of his being, cor-

rupting all the actions of life, making him too wretched to repress his agony, and too degraded to desire reform! Turning from this horrid representation of all who reject the gospel, behold him who died in the faith. Sin has no longer dominion over him. There is nothing now to clog his wings, nothing to weary his mind, nothing to mar his joy. How honored by the presence. how blest in the love of Christ! The Godhead smiles upon him! he wears a crown of rejoicing, he holds the insignia of victory, he sings a new song;—worthy is the Lamb which was slain! With these descriptions, the reality of one of which we must shortly be, I entreat you to abandon those hopes of heaven which are not founded on a fair comparison of your hearts with the conditions of salvation. Rely no longer upon those attributes of God, which instead of affording you protection will make your misery certain and tremendous. Expect pardon without repentance, and you will soon awake to the appalling truth, that you disbelieved the plainest declarations of God; you will awake, but it will be to an unavailing wakefulness. in circumstances where repentance itself can bring no relief, a cry for help no remedy, in circumstances of unknown anguish, of irrepressible bursting agony.

ImTheStory.com

Personalized Classic Books in many genre's

Unique gift for kids, partners, friends, colleagues

Customize:

- Character Names
- Upload your own front/back cover images (optional)
- Inscribe a personal message/dedication on the inside page (optional)

Customize many titles Including
- Alice in Wonderland
- Romeo and Juliet
- The Wizard of Oz
- A Christmas Carol
- Dracula
- Dr. Jekyll & Mr. Hyde
- And more...

WS - #0045 - 220923 - C0 - 229/152/12 - PB - 9781313282079 - Gloss Lamination